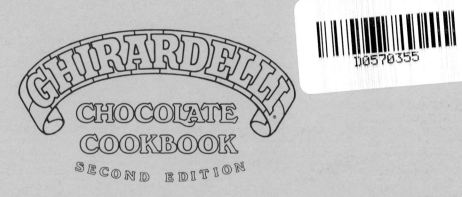

GHIRARDELLI

CHOCOLATE COOKBOOK

SECOND EDITION

FOREWORD

In the *Ghirardelli Original Chocolate Cookbook* you will discover chocolate as a magic flavor ingredient in many unique recipes from beverages to soups and desserts. A touch of chocolate is even found in outstanding main dishes to enhance the flavor and make cooking fun! You will enjoy the great new chocolate experience, cooking with these recipes for breakfast, lunch, and dinner as well as entertaining. You can even have a gourmet dinner with chocolate in every course! Have fun cooking with Ghirardelli Chocolate.

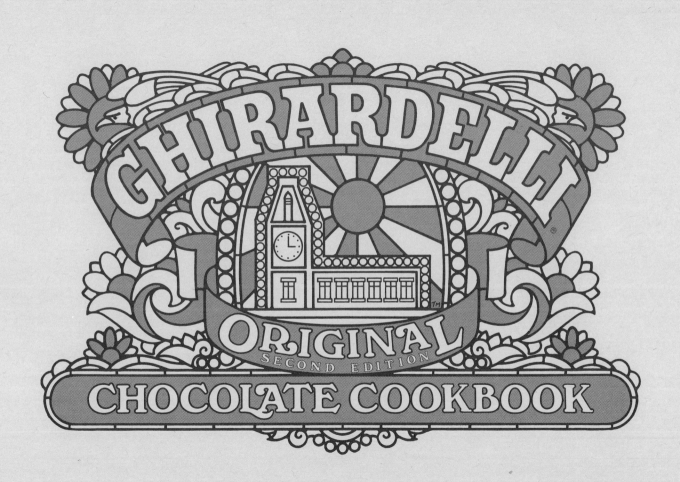

GHIRARDELLI

ORIGINAL
SECOND EDITION

CHOCOLATE COOKBOOK

4

Published by Ghirardelli Chocolate Company
1111 139th Avenue, San Leandro, California 94578

Printed in the United States of America.

Author: Phyllis Larsen

Illustrator: Sylvia R. Giblin

Book Design: Dana Levy

Typographer: Vera Allen Composition
               Castro Valley, California

Printing: Mariposa Press
            Concord, California

ISBN 0-9610218-0-2

CONTENTS

GHIRARDELLI

INTRODUCTION

Chocolate tastes are changing! That was our conclusion after reading through the hundreds of recipe requests Ghirardelli receives every year. While the old favorites - chocolate chip cookies, chocolate cake, and hot chocolate - still rank right up at the top, chocolate enthusiasts have begun to demand more adventure and variety from their favorite sweet.

Throughout its long history, the Ghirardelli Company has provided its popular chocolate recipes to the public. In recent years, as the American taste for more sophisticated fare has grown, we have recognized the need for a more encompassing chocolate cookbook that would include both traditional and gourmet dishes. We asked our home economist to help us, and the result is a wide-ranging collection of baking and cooking recipes that will take you from breakfast to dinner, and from soup through dessert - all in one book.

We have kept the old favorites, added distinctive flavors to familiar dishes, and created many exciting and new ways to use Ghirardelli Chocolate. The recipes included in this collection have been thoroughly tested in our kitchens. They are easy to prepare, and, although often exotic in taste, are made with ingredients readily available in neighborhood supermarkets.

As you leaf through the book, you will notice that our home economist experimented with basic recipes. By adding small amounts of Ghirardelli Ground Chocolate to soups, sauces, and gravies, she succeeded in delicately altering the flavors and in enriching the colors of everyday dishes.

These recipes are just a sampling of the endless variations that an unfettered imagination can bring to cooking and baking with Ghirardelli Chocolate. We hope they inspire you to try your own hand at experimenting with heretofore unimaginable combinations of flavors. Give your creativity full rein, and discover how Ghirardelli Chocolate can be the nicest ingredient that ever happened to your daily meals.

THE GHIRARDELLI CHOCOLATE COMPANY

A Piece of San Francisco History

The history of the Ghirardelli Chocolate Company is so closely interlaced with the growth of San Francisco, that it is impossible to become informed about the company without learning something about the city. The block of Victorian buildings on North Point Street, today the landmark restaurant and shopping complex known as Ghirardelli Square, was the last San Francisco home of the Ghirardelli Chocolate Factory. The story of how Domingo Ghirardelli became one of the chocolate barons of the West ranks as one of the most fascinating business sagas in San Francisco history.

Domingo Ghirardelli was introduced to the art of chocolate making as a young boy in Rapallo, Italy. By the age of 20, he had already begun to establish himself in the chocolate trade when he opened his first confection shop in Lima, Peru. Fortuitously, the shop next door was occupied by a cabinetmaker from Philadelphia, James Lick, a man who was also fated to play an important role in California history. The time was the late 1840's, and the fantastic tales of the Gold Rush had raced around the world. James Lick, excited by the opportunities for wealth and adventure, packed up his belongings - and, with great foresight, 600 pounds of Ghirardelli's chocolate - and set sail for California.

In 1848, San Francisco was a frontier town of make-shift dwellings, largely occupied by transient miners with visions of gold dancing before their eyes. Basic goods were in short supply, and luxuries, such as chocolate, were almost non-existent. Lick, always quick to spot a business opportunity, wrote to his friend Ghirardelli and urged him to come to California.

Soon after arriving in San Francisco in 1849, Ghirardelli opened his first general store in Stockton, and, a few months later, a second store in San Francisco. Business advanced so briskly that within the year, Ghirardelli was the owner of a fleet of sloops-which he used to transport his merchandise along the San Joaquin River, the proprietor of the Europa Hotel -

one of the first erected in San Francisco, and a rich man with $25,000 to his name.

In those days, fortunes were made and lost virtually overnight, and Ghirardelli did both. In two strokes of bad luck, his warehouses in Stockton and in San Francisco were destroyed by fire - both within four days.

Less resilient men would have been defeated by such a business catastrophe, but Ghirardelli, taking his remaining savings, returned to his original trade, chocolate making, and opened a shop on Kearny and Washington. His lucky touch returned, and as his business began to thrive, he moved to larger and larger quarters, eventually settling at 415-17 Jackson Street, the site of the Ghirardelli Chocolate Factory for the next 40 years. Luckily, the Jackson Square neighborhood was spared the ravages of the 1906 earthquake, and today, the building that housed the first large Ghirardelli Chocolate Manufactury is still standing.

By the 1880's, the Ghirardelli Chocolate Company was one of the largest in the West, selling over 50,000 pounds a year. The mainstay of the business was the ground chocolate, which was manufactured by a process Ghirardelli himself had invented and patented.

Having outgrown the Jackson Street location, Ghirardelli searched for a new site with sufficient space for expansion. He selected one of the prime spots in the city, one square block on North Point, overlooking the San Francisco Bay. Embarking on a spectacular 11 year building project with his sons, they constructed the buildings that became the headquarters for Ghirardelli Chocolate for more than half a century.

In 1962, the Ghirardelli Chocolate Company was bought by the Golden Grain Macaroni Company. The North Point buildings, while charming in appearance, were no longer adequate to produce the large quantities of chocolate consumers were demanding. The new owners built a large and modern plant in San Leandro, and in 1966, it became the new home of the Ghirardelli Chocolate Company.

Today, in the original red brick buildings that housed the Chocolate Factory, you can visit unique shops and dine in a diversity of gourmet restaurants. Be sure to stop at the Ghirardelli Chocolate Manufactory and Soda Fountain and see for yourself how chocolate is made. Visit us at Ghirardelli Square for unique chocolate gifts and perhaps enjoy one of our famous hot fudge sundaes.

COOKING WITH CHOCOLATE
Products used in this Cookbook

GROUND CHOCOLATE AND COCOA
An exclusive GHIRARDELLI product. This is a special dry chocolate mix containing sugar and vanilla flavoring. Originally produced to make the perfect cup of hot chocolate with the addition of hot milk, the product has been expanded to be used for cakes, pies, desserts and main dishes. Do not substitute any other product for GROUND CHOCOLATE in recipes in this book. Packed: 1 lb. box, 3-lb. can.

INSTANT CHOCOLATE FLAVOR DRINK
Sweetened chocolate mix to be used with hot or cold milk for beverages and some other recipes. Packed: 1 lb. box.

SEMI-SWEET CHOCOLATE CHIPS
Bits of chocolate used for cookies or desserts. Packed: 6 oz. or 12 oz. bags.

SEMI-SWEET CHOCOLATE BAR
Highest quality for baking, desserts and eating. Marked into 8 (½ ounce) sections. Use 2 sections for each ounce specified in recipe. Packed: 4 oz. bar.

SWEET COOKING CHOCOLATE BAR
Slightly sweeter than semi-sweet chocolate. Used for German Chocolate Cake, desserts and eating. Marked into 8 (½ ounce) sections. Use 2 sections for each ounce specified in recipe. Packed: 4 oz. bar.

MILK CHOCOLATE BLOCKS
Delicious milk chocolate for candy, frosting and eating. Most frequently used for Rocky Road Candy and Hot Fudge Sauce recipes. This large bar is scored into 10 (1 ounce) squares. Packed: 10 oz. bar.

UNSWEETENED BAKING CHOCOLATE
Straight chocolate, no sugar added. Used for baking and desserts only. Marked into 8 (½ ounce) sections. Use 2 sections for each ounce specified in recipe. Packed: 4 oz. bar.

MINT WAFERS
Round, flat wafers made of solid, semi-sweet, mint-flavored chocolate. Good for special cookies and eating. Packed: 5 oz. box or in bulk.

FLICK-ETTES
Chocolate flavored baking bits used mostly for chocolate chip cookies. Made with vegetable oil rather than cocoa butter. Sweeter, with less chocolate flavor than real chocolate chips. More economical than real chocolate chips. Mint chocolate flavor also available. Packed: 12 oz. bag.

Best Ways to Melt Chocolate

For best results, always use the proper method of melting chocolate. The temperature of melted chocolate should be lukewarm, about 110–120°F. It should feel slightly warm — not hot — to your fingers. Stir constantly to melt chocolate evenly and quickly. Remove from heat as soon as chocolate is smoothly melted.

DOUBLE BOILER

Start by breaking the chocolate into very small uniform pieces and placing it in double boiler. Use only 1 inch of water in the bottom part of the pan. The water should not touch the top pan and should be simmering gently, not boiling. The delicate chocolate will melt in the heat from the steam. Stir chocolate constantly as it melts. Partially melted chocolate will continue to melt after removal from heat. Stir until smooth.

To melt small amounts of chocolate, place in small container in pan of hot water (1/2 inch deep) on low heat.

HEAVY SAUCEPAN

Chocolate may be melted in a heavy saucepan on low heat. Stir constantly while melting. Use this method if chocolate is combined with other ingredients such as butter, syrup or two or more tablespoons of liquid.

OVEN MELTING

Place chocolate in small container. Preheat oven, then turn off heat. Check frequently while chocolate is melting.

MICROWAVE OVEN

Microwave ovens are great for melting chocolate. Always melt chocolate in glass or special plastic containers. Since microwave ovens vary by brand and model, it is best to follow the individual manufacturer's suggested instructions for melting chocolate. You should experiment carefully and check frequently until you are used to melting chocolate. The temperature of melted chocolate should be only 110–120°F or lukewarm when touched.

When chocolate melts in microwave, it retains its original shape. It will not look melted; you must stir it to see if it has really melted. Check frequently so the chocolate does not become too hot and burn or get stiff or lumpy. Generally, when chocolate is melted by itself, you may use HIGH or MEDIUM (about 500 watts) for 2–3 minutes, depending upon the amount of chocolate and your type of oven. Check melting chocolate after 1 minute and then every 30 seconds. When chocolate is melted with shortening, proceed with the same method.

When chocolate is melted with liquid such as milk or water, use MEDIUM or LOW for 2–4 minutes or the liquid will boil before the chocolate melts. Stir hard to blend ingredients with chocolate and produce a smooth mixture.

Milk chocolate is more sensitive to heat than semi-sweet or baking chocolate. Use MEDIUM or LOW for 2–3 minutes. If melted chocolate appears to have small lumps, stir constantly until smooth; do not reheat. Too much heat will thicken rather than melt milk chocolate.

MELTING CHOCOLATE CHIPS

Chocolate chips are specially formulated by GHIRARDELLI to retain their shape in the heat of the oven for cookie baking. They will not melt as smoothly as milk or semi-sweet chocolate bars. Melted chocolate chips may be used in cake recipes, but they are not recommended for dipping chocolate.

CHOCOLATE FLAVORED BAKING CHIPS

Use the same methods to melt chocolate flavored Flick-ettes. Flick-ettes are made from a compound chocolate, which does not melt as smoothly and is a thicker consistency than real chocolate. Compound chocolate contains vegetable shortening in place of cocoa butter. Flick-ettes are sweeter than semi-sweet chocolate chips. When melted Flick-ettes are used in a recipe, the product will be lighter in color, sweeter and have less chocolate flavor than when real chocolate is used.

Problems in Melting Chocolate

There are only two factors that prevent chocolate from melting properly: too much heat or a small amount of liquid mixed with the chocolate.

It is important to follow accepted methods of melting chocolate. If too high a heat is used, the chocolate will stiffen. In other words, too much heat will actually thicken chocolate rather than melt it. If this occurs, try adding hot water. Stir in up to ¼ cup of water, 1 tablespoon at a time. If lumpy, stir with wire whisk.

The pan used to melt chocolate must be very dry. If it has just been washed, dry thoroughly with paper towel. A few drops of water in the pan will actually stiffen the chocolate into a ball. If this occurs, try adding hot water. Stir in up to ¼ cup of water, 1 tablespoon at a time. You can add 2 tablespoons or more of liquid when melting chocolate, but you cannot add a very small amount of liquid.

"Tempering" Chocolate for Dipping

Dipping chocolate is serious business that requires knowledge, patience and practice. Chocolates should not be dipped in hot summer weather. The room temperature should be 70°F or less.

When melting chocolate for coating or dipping, it is very important that the temperature be carefully controlled. If the temperature is not regulated, the chocolate will harden with a "bloom," white oil markings on the surface. The flavor is still good, but the candy has an undesirable appearance and texture. Tempering is necessary because the cellular structure of the cocoa butter disappears when chocolate melts and becomes smooth. The cells have to be slowly built up again, so the chocolate sets properly.

For dipping, always use highest quality chocolate. Do not use chocolate chips, which are formulated to hold their shape in cookie baking. GHIRARDELLI MILK CHOCOLATE BLOCKS or SEMI-SWEET CHOCOLATE are good products for dipping. It is easier for a beginner to dip Semi-Sweet Chocolate than Milk Chocolate.

Using a double boiler, carefully follow directions listed in the section, "How to Melt Chocolate." A good method for breaking thick chocolate into small uniform pieces is to use an ice pick or thin screwdriver on a wooden cutting board. Thin chocolate may be chopped into tiny cubes with a long knife.

EASY TEMPERING METHOD

Starting with a pound of chocolate, break up ⅔ and melt in a double boiler. Melt just until the chocolate is liquid and smooth (110–120°F). When it is smooth, add the remaining ⅓ broken chocolate. Turn off heat and stir until it all becomes smooth again.

With this technique, the chocolate is heated, brought down to a lower temperature with the addition of the unmelted chocolate, then reheated. When it is smooth, the chocolate is ready to be used for dipping or other decorations.

Allow dipped chocolates to cool completely. Store in a cool, dry place. The ideal storage temperature is 65–70°F.

A good place to store finished chocolates is an unheated closet or garage.

Leftover melted chocolate can be made into easy drop candies. Warm chocolate slightly and stir in any combination of nuts, miniature marshmallows, crisp cereal, raisins, coconut or chow mein noodles. Drop by teaspoon or pour into pan and cut into squares.

Storage Conditions for Chocolate

Temperature greatly affects all chocolate products. Chocolate should be stored in a dry, cool place below 75°F. Do not refrigerate chocolate unless the room temperature is above 75°F and the chocolate would melt anyway. Never freeze chocolate!

If chocolate has melted and then hardened again, the cocoa butter will come to the surface and appear as white markings. Unless the chocolate has cream centers, it can be remelted for cooking or baking. The product tastes fine but has an undesirable appearance.

When transporting chocolate, remember that a closed car or trunk becomes very hot. This is not a proper place to store chocolate. Do not send gifts of chocolate during the hot summer months. Chocolate will melt in the mail if it travels in and out of high temperatures. Even if it is not hot where you live, consider what the temperature might be along the entire route the chocolate gift must follow.

Ingredients Used for Recipes in this Cookbook

Standard measuring spoons and cups were used with level measurements.

Eggs used were large size, not extra large or jumbo.

Pure vanilla extract was used, not vanillin or artificial vanilla.

Butter or margarine was cubed, not in tub or soft whipped.

Regular salted butter was used, not sweet butter.

Flour was all purpose, bleached, unless cake flour is indicated.

Baking powder was regular double acting.

Light brown sugar was packed down before measuring.

Chocolate products were GHIRARDELLI brand only.

Electric and gas ranges were used for recipe testing.

The oven was preheated to the correct temperature before baking.

Microwave recipes were tested in 500 and 700 watt ovens.

Baked goods, such as cookies and cakes, were prepared with an electric mixer.

A food processor was used to chop and grate ingredients and combine crust mixtures.

Decorating with Chocolate

CHOCOLATE CURLS

Semi-Sweet or Milk Chocolate may be used for chocolate curls. The chocolate should be slightly warmed by holding it in your hand. Using a vegetable peeler, draw the sharp blade quickly along the surface of the chocolate, forming a round curl. For wide curls, use diagonal cuts on the chocolate. It is best to make the curl and drop directly onto cake, pie or whipped cream. The curls are too fragile to be made in advance. Curls take a little practice, but the technique is not hard to master.

GRATED CHOCOLATE

Semi-Sweet or Milk Chocolate may be used for grating. For best results, chocolate and grater should be chilled first. Quickly grate chocolate directly onto cake, pie, or whipped cream for decoration. This is the easiest chocolate decoration.

Chocolate can also be grated with a food processor. Using the cutter blade, break up chocolate into the bowl of processor. Process until chocolate is finely grated.

MOLDED CHOCOLATE

Small metal and plastic molds are available in kitchen specialty stores and by mail order. Flick-ettes Mint Chocolate Flavored Chips are ideal for molding because they do not have to be tempered. GHIRARDELLI SEMI-SWEET CHOCOLATE may also be used. Break up chocolate. Carefully melt ⅔ of the chocolate. Remove from heat and stir in remaining chocolate, finely chopped. Spread chocolate into molds; smooth surface with small metal spatula. Chill until firm. Let stand at room temperature a few minutes before removal from mold. Handle molded chocolate as little as possible. Use as decoration for cakes or pies.

CHOCOLATE STARS

GHIRARDELLI CHOCOLATE STARS and NON-PAREILS may be used to decorate cookies before baking and cupcakes after frosting.

Be an Artist with Chocolate

CHOCOLATE PUTTY FOR DECORATIONS

1 bar (4 oz.) GHIRARDELLI SEMI-SWEET CHOCOLATE
1 tablespoon light corn syrup

In double boiler, melt broken chocolate, stirring constantly, or microwave on MEDIUM for 2–3 minutes, stirring until smooth. Remove from heat. Stir in corn syrup. Pour mixture into flat pan lined with waxed paper. Chill 15–20 minutes or until firm.

The decorating technique is not hard but it may take practice to become perfect. It is important that the decorating chocolate is the right temperature. If it is too hard, let soften at room temperature. If too soft, chill longer.

Chocolate Roses

Press chilled Chocolate Putty into a ball. Divide into 4 sections. Knead each section slightly and roll into a 5-inch rod. Cut into 16 slices. Work on a double piece of waxed paper. Using 1 small slice, form a cone shape with your fingers. Flatten cone on bottom and press onto waxed paper. With a small metal spatula spread each slice thin to form a rose petal. Shape each chocolate petal around cone. Make a thin rod for a stem, cutting small slits for thorn marks. Cut off bottom of rose, using this excess for leaves. With rolling pin, flatten excess chocolate for leaves. Use a small knife to cut out leaves. Arrange stem, roses and leaves on top of cake for decorations. Roses may be made in advance and kept refrigerated. Makes 4 large roses.

Chocolate Cutouts

Place Chocolate Putty in heavy plastic bag. With rolling pin, flatten chocolate as thin as possible. Cut bag, removing top piece of plastic. Press small metal decorating cutters into chocolate. Chill 5 minutes for easy removal from plastic. Decorate cakes for special events or holidays. Cutouts may also be served like cookies with desserts. Use your imagination to decorate with chocolate.

DECORATIVE CHOCOLATE LEAVES

Select leaves that are stiff and smooth such as camellia, citrus or ivy. Clean with cold water; dry with paper towels. Break up 1 bar (4 oz.) GHIRARDELLI SEMI-SWEET CHOCOLATE. In heavy saucepan on low heat, melt chocolate with 2 teaspoons vegetable shortening, stirring constantly. Remove from heat. Cool slightly until chocolate is thick and cool to the touch.

With one hand hold leaf by stem with fingers supporting under leaf. The leaf should be held underside up. With small metal spatula, paint chocolate thickly on underside of leaf. Place on waxed paper on baking sheet. Chill 1 hour or until very hard. Carefully peel off leaf. Use as decoration on top of frosted cakes, ice cream or other desserts. Makes about 20 leaves.

DARK CHOCOLATE GLAZE
FROSTING FOR DECORATING
2 bars (4 oz. each) GHIRARDELLI SEMI-SWEET CHOCOLATE
3 Tablespoons water.

In double boiler, melt broken chocolate; remove from heat. With wire whip, stir in water, beating until smooth and shiny. Spread over top and sides of cake. Frosting may be used in small pastry tube for cake decorating. Allow frosting to firm in cool place. (Do not refrigerate or frosting will lose its gloss.)

GLOSSARY OF CHOCOLATE

CACAO (COCOA) BEANS:
Source of cocoa and chocolate, cacao beans are the fruit of the cacao tree, which grows chiefly in West Africa and Latin America.

CACAO NIBS:
The "meat" of the cacao bean. After the beans are cleaned and roasted at controlled temperature to bring out full flavor and aroma, the outer shells are removed, leaving the nibs.

CHOCOLATE LIQUOR:
Base material of all chocolate products. The nibs, which contain more than 50% cocoa butter, are ground by a process which generates enough heat to liquify the cocoa butter and form what is known as "chocolate liquor."

COCOA BUTTER:
The unique vegetable fat extracted from the chocolate liquor under high pressure.

BITTER CHOCOLATE:
(Commonly referred to also as unsweetened, baking, or cooking chocolate.) Chocolate liquor which has been cooled and molded, usually in bars.

SWEET CHOCOLATE:
Combination of bitter chocolate, sugar, a little vanilla, and cocoa butter. Usually packed in bar form.

SEMI-SWEET CHOCOLATE:
Made by adding cocoa butter and sugar to chocolate liquor, as in sweet chocolate. After thorough mixing, the finished chocolate is cooled and molded into bars and chocolate chips.

MILK CHOCOLATE:
The most favored chocolate for eating. Milk chocolate is a combination of chocolate liquor, added cocoa butter, sugar, milk or cream, and a little vanilla. The processing is essentially the same as that for sweet and semi-sweet chocolate.

COCOA POWDER:
The portion of chocolate solids that remains after most of the cocoa butter has been expressed.

BREAKFAST COCOA:
High fat cocoa powder with at least 22% cocoa butter.

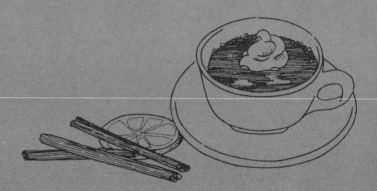

A basic sauce for chocolate drinks from Ghirardelli Square . . .

GOLDEN GATE CHOCOLATE SAUCE

1⅓ cups GHIRARDELLI GROUND
   CHOCOLATE
1 cup sugar
Pinch of salt
1 cup hot water
1 teaspoon vanilla

In saucepan, combine Ground Chocolate, sugar and salt. Add hot water, stirring until chocolate is dissolved. Heat to boiling; lower heat and cook five minutes without stirring again. Remove from heat, add vanilla. Serve hot or cold over your favorite ice cream, cake or pudding. This basic sauce is also used to make hot or cold beverages. Makes two cups sauce.

Soda fountain at home . . .

CHOCOLATE MILK SHAKE

1 cup vanilla or chocolate ice cream
¼ cup milk
2 tablespoons Golden Gate
   Chocolate Sauce
(Recipe above)

In blender, combine all ingredients. Mix at low speed until smooth. For Malted Milk Shake, add 1 tablespoon malted milk. Makes 1 serving.

CHOCOLATE ICE-CREAM SODA

1 heaping tablespoon GHIRARDELLI
  INSTANT CHOCOLATE FLAVOR
  DRINK
½ cup milk
1 scoop vanilla or chocolate ice
  cream
Chilled soda water

In a tall glass, stir Instant Chocolate Flavor Drink with milk. Add ice cream. Fill glass slowly with chilled soda water. Makes 1 serving.

24

HOT CHOCOLATE À LA MODE

¾ cup milk
1 heaping tablespoon GHIRARDELLI
  GROUND CHOCOLATE
Vanilla ice cream

For each serving, combine milk with Ground Chocolate in a saucepan. Heat, whipping until foamy. Pour into preheated mug. Top with small scoop of vanilla ice cream.

SUMMERTIME CHOCOLATE EGGNOG

¾ cup milk
1 egg
1 heaping tablespoon GHIRARDELLI
  INSTANT CHOCOLATE FLAVOR
  DRINK
¼ teaspoon vanilla
Dash of salt
Dash of nutmeg

In blender, combine ingredients; mix until smooth. Makes 1 serving.

CHOCOLATE BREAKFAST DRINK

1 cup milk
1 egg
1 ripe banana, cut up
2 heaping tablespoons GHIRARDELLI
  INSTANT CHOCOLATE FLAVOR
  DRINK

In blender, combine all ingredients; mix at low speed until smooth. For Malted Milk Breakfast Drink, add 1 tablespoon malted milk. Makes 1 serving.

Delicious hot beverages . . .

HOT CHOCOLATE FOR A PARTY

1 pound (3½ cups) GHIRARDELLI GROUND CHOCOLATE
1 gallon milk

Heat milk. Add Ground Chocolate and stir to blend. Makes 25 (¾ cup) servings.

For campers or dieters . . .

EASY HOT CHOCOLATE MIX

26

1 cup GHIRARDELLI GROUND CHOCOLATE
1½ cups nonfat dry milk

Mix Ground Chocolate with dry milk. Store dry mixture in can or heavy plastic bag. To make hot chocolate, fill each mug half full of chocolate mix. Stir in boiling water. Top with marshmallows, if desired. A handy mix for camping trips or for easy, low-calorie hot chocolate at home. Makes 8 servings.

HOT MOCHA NIGHTCAP

¾ cup ground coffee
¼ cup GHIRARDELLI GROUND CHOCOLATE
5 cups cold water

Combine coffee and Ground Chocolate. In your favorite coffee maker, prepare Hot Mocha beverage using coffee-chocolate mixture with water. Serve with whipped cream, if desired. Makes 4 servings.

Company beverages . . .

MONTEZUMA'S HOT CHOCOLATE

3 cups milk
½ cup GHIRARDELLI GROUND
   CHOCOLATE
⅛ teaspoon cinnamon

In saucepan, combine all ingredients. Heat, whipping until very foamy. Pour into preheated mugs. Serve with stick of cinnamon, if desired. Makes 4 servings.

P.M. MOCHA DEMITASSE

3 cups cold water
½ cup ground coffee
3 whole cloves
2 bay leaves
Peeling from one whole orange
4 drops Angostura bitters
3 tablespoons GHIRARDELLI
   GROUND CHOCOLATE

Fill drip coffee maker with water. Combine remaining ingredients in top basket. Proceed as you would to make coffee. Serve with lemon peel or whipped cream and a sprinkle of nutmeg. Makes 6 demitasse.

Chilled instant drinks for parties . . .

HOLIDAY BRANDY EGGNOG

2 cups milk
⅔ cup GHIRARDELLI INSTANT
   CHOCOLATE FLAVOR DRINK
4 eggs
½ cup brandy
Pinch of nutmeg
2 cups half and half

In blender, combine milk, Instant Chocolate Flavor Drink, eggs, brandy and nutmeg; mix until smooth. Add half and half. Pour into chilled punch bowl. Decorate with whipped cream, if desired. Makes 8 (¾ cup) servings.

Hot Chocolate drinks with a punch . . .

MONTGOMERY STREET BRACER

¾ cup milk
3 tablespoons Kahlua or coffee
   liqueur
1 heaping tablespoon GHIRARDELLI
   GROUND CHOCOLATE
1 tablespoon half and half

For each serving, combine ingredients in a saucepan. Heat, whipping until foamy. Pour into preheated mug. Top with whipped cream, if desired.

Hot Chocolate drinks to warm the heart...

BRANDIED CHOCO-LATE

¾ **cup milk**
1 **heaping tablespoon** GHIRARDELLI
  GROUND CHOCOLATE
1 **tablespoon brandy**

For each serving, combine ingredients in a saucepan. Heat, whipping until foamy. Pour into preheated mug. Top with whipped cream, if desired.

HOT CHOCOLATE AT SUNSET

¾ **cup milk**
1 **heaping tablespoon** GHIRARDELLI
  GROUND CHOCOLATE
1 **tablespoon Curaçao or orange**
  liqueur

For each serving, combine ingredients in a saucepan. Heat, whipping until foamy. Pour into preheated mug. Garnish with whipped cream and top with twist of orange, if desired.

IRISH CHOCOLATE S.F.

¾ **cup milk**
1 **heaping tablespoon** GHIRARDELLI
  GROUND CHOCOLATE
2 **tablespoons Irish whiskey**
Whipped cream

For each serving, combine ingredients in saucepan. Heat, whipping until foamy. Add Irish whiskey. Pour into preheated mug. Top with whipped cream.

Hot chocolate drinks with a kick . . .

CALIFORNIA CAPPUCCINO

¾ cup milk
1 heaping tablespoon GHIRARDELLI
  GROUND CHOCOLATE
1 teaspoon instant coffee
1 tablespoon brandy

For each serving, combine ingredients in a saucepan. Heat, whipping until foamy. Pour into preheated mug. Top with whipped cream, if desired.

SWEDISH GLÖGG CHOKLAD

1 fifth Burgundy wine
1 fifth ruby port wine
½ cup raisins
¼ cup whole almonds
¼ cup sugar
2 tablespoons GHIRARDELLI
  GROUND CHOCOLATE
2 cinnamon sticks
1 tablespoon orange marmalade
10 whole cloves
10 cardamom seeds, peeled
Dash Angostura bitters
2 tablespoons brandy

In large pot, combine Burgundy, port, raisins, almonds, sugar, Ground Chocolate, cinnamon and marmalade. Place cloves and cardamom into tea ball; drop into wine mixture. Simmer, covered, 30 minutes. Add bitters and brandy. Glögg may be prepared in advance and reheated for the party. Makes 12 (½ cup) servings.

The Aztecs added a tincture of achiotl . . .

HOME BREW MOCHA LIQUEUR

3 cups sugar
1½ cups GHIRARDELLI GROUND
    CHOCOLATE
2 tablespoons instant coffee
2 cups boiling water
1 fifth vodka
1 vanilla bean, cut into pieces

Dissolve sugar, Ground Chocolate and coffee in boiling water. Stir in vodka and vanilla bean. Pour into jars. Store, covered, in cool, dark place for one month; shake once a week. Serve as after-dinner liqueur or as a dessert sauce or over ice cream. Makes 1½ quarts liqueur.

Brandy Mocha Liqueur
Add 1 pint brandy to Home Brew Mocha Liqueur recipe above. For individual service, add 2 tablespoons brandy to each ¼ cup Home Brew Mocha Liqueur.

AMBER ANGEL COCKTAIL

2 tablespoons Home Brew Mocha
    Liqueur (Recipe above)
2 tablespoons brandy
2 tablespoons half and half

For each cocktail, mix all ingredients together. Serve in cordial glass over ice.

Start your day with chocolate . . .

EMBARCADERO CHOCOLATE PANCAKES

1 cup water
¼ cup GHIRARDELLI GROUND CHOCOLATE
Dash nutmeg
Dash cinnamon
1½ cups complete buttermilk pancake mix

With wire whip, blend water with Ground Chocolate, nutmeg and cinnamon. Add pancake mix; beat until smooth. Let stand 5 minutes to thicken batter. Pour batter onto oiled hot griddle or 400°F electric skillet. Turn pancakes when bubbles form on top. Makes 15 pancakes.

CHOCOLATE MAPLE SYRUP

In saucepan, combine 1 cup maple flavor syrup, 3 tablespoons Ghirardelli Ground Chocolate and 2 tablespoons butter. Heat to boiling; blend with wire whip. Serve warm over pancakes.

34

A unique breakfast treat . . .

BAYSHORE CHOCOLATE WAFFLES

1 bar (4 oz.) GHIRARDELLI SEMI-
   SWEET CHOCOLATE
¼ cup butter or margarine
2 cups flour
3 teaspoons baking powder
Pinch nutmeg
Pinch cinnamon
Pinch ground cardamom
½ cup chopped pecans
3 eggs, separated
1½ cups milk
½ cup half and half
1 teaspoon vanilla
¼ teaspoon salt
¼ cup sugar

In heavy saucepan, break chocolate and melt with butter. Into large bowl, sift flour, baking powder, nutmeg, cinnamon and cardamom; add nuts. Beat egg yolks with milk, half and half and vanilla. Mix liquid with dry ingredients, beating until smooth. Beat egg whites with salt until soft mounds form. Gradually add sugar, beating until stiff peaks form. Fold egg whites into batter. Preheat greased waffle iron. Bake waffles according to manufacturer's directions. Serve with warm Chocolate Maple Syrup (page 34). Makes 4 large waffles.

CHOCOLATE DESSERT WAFFLES

Bayshore Chocolate Waffles may be prepared in advance and frozen or refrigerated until ready to serve. Reheat waffles on oven rack for 5 minutes, using moderate heat. Spoon vanilla ice cream over each waffle. Top with warm Chocolate Maple Syrup (page 34).

New chocolate twist to traditional oatmeal . . .

OATMEAL BREAKFAST TREAT

3 cups water
⅓ cup GHIRARDELLI INSTANT
    CHOCOLATE FLAVOR DRINK
⅓ cup raisins
1 tablespoon butter or margarine
½ teaspoon salt
1½ cups rolled oats

Heat water to boiling with Instant Chocolate Flavor Drink, raisins, butter and salt. Stir in rolled oats, cooking as directed on package. Remove from heat; cover and let stand a few minutes. Serve with milk or cream, if desired. Makes 4 (¾ cup) servings.

36

TEA TIME TOASTIES

6 slices white bread
3 tablespoons butter or margarine,
    softened
2 tablespoons GHIRARDELLI
    GROUND CHOCOLATE
2 tablespoons sugar
½ teaspoon cinnamon
2 tablespoons finely chopped nuts

Trim crusts off bread. Flatten each slice with rolling pin. Butter one side of bread. Place on cookie sheet butter side down. Blend remaining butter with Ground Chocolate, sugar and cinnamon. Spread chocolate mixture on top side of bread. Sprinkle with nuts. Roll up each slice, butter side out. Bake at 450°F for 5 minutes or until golden brown. Makes 6 servings.

Shake up your day with this chocolate coffee cake ...

EARTHQUAKE COFFEE CAKE

Coffee Cake
⅓ cup GHIRARDELLI GROUND
   CHOCOLATE
¼ cup sugar
½ teaspoon instant coffee
2 cups buttermilk baking mix
1 egg
½ cup sour cream
½ cup half and half

Topping
⅓ cup buttermilk baking mix
2 tablespoons GHIRARDELLI
   GROUND CHOCOLATE
3 tablespoons packed brown sugar
½ teaspoon cinnamon
2 tablespoons butter or margarine
2 tablespoons sliced almonds

Cake
In bowl, blend together Ground Chocolate, sugar and coffee. Stir in baking mix. Beat egg with sour cream and half and half; add to dry ingredients. Stir lightly to combine ingredients. (Do not overmix.) Spread into greased 9 by 1½-inch round cake pan.

Topping
Combine baking mix, Ground Chocolate, sugar and cinnamon. With pastry blender, cut in butter. Sprinkle over top of cake batter. Run knife through topping and batter in a swirl pattern for earthquake marbling. Sprinkle with nuts. Bake at 400°F for 25 minutes. Cut into wedges. Serve warm. Makes 8 servings.

37

Poppy seeds accent this Sunday brunch yeast bread . . .

CALIFORNIA POPPY COFFEE CAKE

Coffee Cake
¾ cup sugar
½ cup milk, scalded
2 eggs
½ teaspoon salt
½ teaspoon ground cardamom
½ cup butter or margarine, softened
4½ cups unsifted flour
2 packages active dry yeast
½ cup warm water

Chocolate Filling
1 package (6 oz.) GHIRARDELLI
 SEMI-SWEET CHOCOLATE CHIPS
¼ cup milk
½ teaspoon cinnamon
⅓ cup poppy seeds

Crumb Topping
¼ cup flour
¼ cup sugar
¼ cup butter or margarine
1 teaspoon cinnamon
⅓ cup sliced almonds

Coffee Cake
In a large bowl, combine sugar, scalded milk, eggs, salt and cardamom; beat until smooth. Add butter and 2 cups flour; beat until smooth. Sprinkle yeast into warm water; stir until dissolved. Add yeast liquid and 1 cup flour to dough; beat 3 minutes. Work in remaining 1½ cups flour. Cover; let rise in warm place until doubled, about 1½ hours.

Punch down dough; turn out and knead lightly on floured board. Roll into rectangle. Spread dough with Chocolate Filling and sprinkle with poppy seeds. Roll up, as for jelly roll, starting with wide end. Place seam side down on greased baking sheet. Shape into a ring and press ends together. Cut 2-inch slices and alternate slices to form a fan ring. Sprinkle with Crumb Topping. Cover and let rise about 1 hour or until doubled in bulk. Bake at 350°F for 30–35 minutes. Serve warm or cold.

Chocolate Filling
Melt Chocolate Chips with milk and cinnamon; stir until smooth. Reserve poppy seeds.

Crumb Topping
Combine flour, sugar, butter and cinnamon; mix with fork until crumbly and toss with nuts.

A quick bread with a touch of the Tropics . . .

ANZA VISTA CHOCOLATE BANANA BREAD

½ cup butter or margarine
½ cup sugar
2 eggs
⅔ cup GHIRARDELLI GROUND
   CHOCOLATE
1½ cups mashed ripe bananas
½ cup chopped walnuts
1¾ cups unsifted flour
1 teaspoon baking powder
1 teaspoon baking soda
½ teaspoon salt

Cream butter lightly with sugar; mix in eggs. Add Ground Chocolate, beating until smooth. Mix in bananas and nuts. Sift flour with baking powder, soda and salt. Mixing by hand, add dry ingredients all at once. (Do not overmix.) Grease bottom of 9 by 5-inch loaf pan. Spread batter into pan and bake at 350°F for 55–60 minutes. Cool 15 minutes; remove from pan. Makes one loaf.

CHOCOLATE APPLESAUCE BREAD

Substitute 1½ cups applesauce for bananas in recipe above.

A "toast" to this muffin magic . . .

SHERRY TEA MUFFINS

2 cups unsifted flour
⅓ cup GHIRARDELLI GROUND
  CHOCOLATE
⅓ cup sugar
1 tablespoon baking powder
½ teaspoon salt
½ teaspoon cinnamon
¼ teaspoon nutmeg
½ cup currants
2 eggs
½ cup sweet sherry wine
¼ cup milk
½ cup oil

Into a bowl, sift flour with Ground Chocolate, sugar, baking powder, salt, cinnamon and nutmeg; stir in currants. Make a well in center of dry ingredients. Beat eggs with wine, milk and oil. Add liquid all at once to dry ingredients, stirring only until moistened. (Do not overmix.) Spoon batter into 12 greased muffin cups, ⅔ full. Sprinkle tops with mixture of 2 tablespoons sugar and 1 tablespoon Ground Chocolate. Bake at 375°F for 20 minutes. Makes 12 muffins.

NOTE: Wrap leftover muffins in foil; reheat in oven. Muffins may also be frozen. To reheat in microwave oven, wrap muffins in paper towel; process on HIGH for 30–60 seconds.

40

Spicy golden loaf flecked with chocolate . . .

HALF MOON BAY PUMPKIN BREAD

4 eggs
3 cups sugar
1 cup oil
2 cups canned pumpkin
3 cups flour
2 teaspoons baking soda
2 teaspoons salt
1 teaspoon baking powder
1½ teaspoons cinnamon
¾ teaspoon nutmeg
¾ teaspoon allspice
½ teaspoon ginger
⅔ cup orange juice
½ cup chopped walnuts
1 bar (4 oz.) GHIRARDELLI
   SEMI-SWEET CHOCOLATE

In mixer bowl, combine eggs, sugar and oil; cream on high speed for 5 minutes. On medium speed, blend in pumpkin. Sift flour with baking soda, salt, baking powder and spices. Add dry ingredients alternately with orange juice. Mix until smooth. (Do not overmix.) Grate chocolate. Fold nuts and grated chocolate into batter. Spread into 2 greased 9 by 5-inch loaf pans. Bake at 350°F for 1½ hours. Bread will keep for several days or may be frozen. Serve plain or buttered. A glaze for the top of the loaf may be made by mixing ½ cup powdered sugar, ⅛ teaspoon nutmeg, ⅛ teaspoon cinnamon and 1 tablespoon milk. Makes 2 loaves.

Everyone will love this chocolate brown bread . . .

PANHANDLE GHIRARDELLI CHOCOLATE BREAD

1 cup milk
1¼ cups water
1 envelope active dry yeast
2 tablespoons oil
¼ cup sugar
½ teaspoon vanilla
6 cups unsifted flour
1 cup GHIRARDELLI GROUND
   CHOCOLATE
2 teaspoons salt
1 teaspoon cinnamon

Heat milk with water until lukewarm (105°–115°F). Soften yeast in warm liquid. Stir in oil, sugar and vanilla. Sift flour with Ground Chocolate, salt and cinnamon. Using wooden spoon, add half the dry ingredients to liquid; add remaining dry ingredients 1 cup at a time, beating until dough leaves the side of the bowl. Turn out on lightly floured board and let rest 10 minutes. Knead dough lightly about 10 minutes or until smooth and elastic; add flour to board as needed to keep dough from sticking. Place in greased bowl; turn over to grease top. Cover with damp cloth. Let rise in warm place (75°–80°F) for about 2 hours or until double in bulk. Knead lightly in bowl. Let rise a second time.

Divide dough and shape into 2 loaves. Place in 2 greased 9 by 5-inch loaf pans. Grease tops lightly. Cover and let rise until double in bulk. Place on lower rack in preheated 425°F oven for 5 minutes. Reduce heat to 350°F and bake about 30 minutes or until top is firm. Brush top crust with melted butter. Remove bread from pans and cool on rack away from drafts. Makes 2 loaves.

Serving Suggestions: Toast and spread with softened cream cheese, peanut butter or marmalade. Makes delicious French toast.

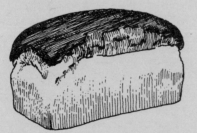

RAISIN CHOCOLATE BREAD

Prepare Panhandle Ghirardelli Chocolate Bread (page 42). For this variation, soak 1 cup raisins in boiling water. Drain well on paper towels. Sprinkle with 1 tablespoon flour. Add to dough in second kneading. Bake as directed.

Chocolate doughnuts to delight family and friends . . .

CHOCOLATE RING-A-DINGS

2 cups unsifted flour
2 teaspoons baking powder
1 teaspoon baking soda
½ teaspoon salt
½ cup GHIRARDELLI GROUND
   CHOCOLATE
½ cup sugar
½ cup milk
¼ cup melted shortening
1 egg

In a bowl, sift together flour, baking powder, baking soda and salt. Combine Ground Chocolate, sugar, milk, cooled shortening and egg; beat until smooth. Add chocolate mixture to dry ingredients, stirring only until flour is moistened. Place dough on board sprinkled with additional ¼ cup flour; lightly knead 2–3 times until soft ball forms. Roll out dough to ¼ inch thick. Cut with floured doughnut cutter; let dry 10 minutes. Deep fat fry in at least 3-inches oil at 375°F for 1½ minutes on each side. Drain on paper towels. Roll in powdered sugar or spread tops with chocolate frosting, if desired. Makes 1 dozen doughnuts.

Smooth, spicy, sherry soup with a pinch of chocolate . . .

SEAL ROCK BLACK BEAN SOUP

1 pound (2 cups) dry black beans
1½ quarts water
1 can (14 oz.) beef broth
1 cup sliced celery
¾ cup chopped onion
½ cup sliced carrots
½ cup diced fresh tomato
1 tablespoon GHIRARDELLI
   GROUND CHOCOLATE
2 teaspoons salt
½ teaspoon dry mustard
¼ teaspoon pepper
¼ teaspoon mace
⅛ teaspoon ground cloves
1 lemon
Dash hot pepper sauce
⅓ cup dry sherry wine

Soak beans overnight; discard water. In stock pot, cook beans with 1½ quarts water, covered, for 1 hour. Add beef broth, celery, onion, carrots, tomato, Ground Chocolate, salt, mustard, pepper, mace and cloves. Squeeze juice from lemon; reserve juice. Add lemon rind to soup pot. Simmer, covered, 1 hour. Remove lemon rind. Purée soup in blender. Add lemon juice and hot pepper sauce. Simmer 15 minutes, stirring frequently. Add sherry; season with salt and pepper. Serve in bowls garnished with thin slices of lemon or chopped hard-cooked eggs, if desired. Makes 2 quarts soup.

47

Vegetable soup with chocolate character . . .

SUTRO HEIGHTS LENTIL SOUP

1 package (12 oz.) lentils
2 quarts water
1 tablespoon GHIRARDELLI
  GROUND CHOCOLATE
1 envelope (1½ oz.) onion soup mix
1 cup chopped celery
1 cup diced carrots
2 lemon slices
2 cloves garlic, minced
2 tablespoons olive oil
¼ teaspoon pepper
1 bay leaf
½ pound smoked sausage, sliced
¼ cup dry sherry wine

In stock pot, combine all ingredients except sausage and wine. Heat to boiling; simmer, covered, for 1 hour. Add sausage and wine. Cook, uncovered, 15 minutes. Season with salt. Garnish each bowl with a thin lemon slice, if desired. Makes 6 (1½ cup) servings.

48

Creamy salad squares dotted with chocolate may be made in advance for easy entertaining . . .

PACIFIC HEIGHTS FROZEN FRUIT SALAD

1 package (6 oz.) cream cheese,
   softened
¼ cup sugar
½ pint whipping cream
1 can (8 oz.) crushed pineapple
¼ cup quartered maraschino cherries
½ of 4 oz. bar (4 sections)
   GHIRARDELLI SEMI-SWEET
   CHOCOLATE
Lettuce leaves
Sour cream

Whip cream cheese with sugar. Gradually add whipping cream, beating until thick and smooth. Grate chocolate. Fold in pineapple, cherries and grated chocolate. Spread into 9 by 5-inch loaf pan. Cover with foil. Freeze 2 hours or until firm. Remove 10 minutes before serving. Cut into squares. Serve on lettuce leaf. Top with sour cream thinned with small amount of maraschino cherry syrup. Makes 4 servings.

Golden yams in sugar and spice . . .

YERBA BUENA FANCY YAMS

2 pounds (4 medium) yams
¼ cup butter or margarine
1 teaspoon salt
½ cup light corn syrup
1 tablespoon GHIRARDELLI
   GROUND CHOCOLATE
½ teaspoon pumpkin pie spice
3 tablespoons Grand Marnier or
   brandy
¼ cup pecan halves

Peel yams; cut into 1-inch slices. in large skillet, brown yams in melted butter; sprinkle with salt while cooking. Blend corn syrup with Ground Chocolate, pumpkin pie spice and Grand Marnier; pour over yams. Sprinkle with nuts. Simmer, covered, 30 minutes. Makes 6 servings.

Serve a pot of beans at your next barbecue . . .

BARBARY COAST BAKED BEANS

1 pound dry white beans
½ pound bacon, diced
¾ cup chopped onion
1 cup barbecue sauce
¼ cup GHIRARDELLI GROUND
    CHOCOLATE
¼ cup packed dark brown sugar
2 tablespoons molasses
½ teaspoon dry mustard
¼ teaspoon pepper
Pinch ground cloves

Soak beans in cold water overnight; drain. Add 4 cups cold water to soaked beans. Simmer, covered, 45–60 minutes or until beans are tender. Drain beans, reserving liquid. Sauté bacon with onion. Add remaining ingredients and 1½ cups reserved bean liquid. Mix with cooked beans in 2½ quart casserole. Bake, covered, at 325° F for 1 hour, stirring occasionally. Uncover and continue baking 1 hour. Makes 6–8 servings.

53

Chocolate brings out the flavor in this prize-winning recipe . . .

WESTERN CHILI CON CHOCOLATE

4 slices bacon, diced
2 tablespoons oil
1 cup chopped onion
1 pound lean ground beef
1 can (28 oz.) tomatoes, crushed
1–3 tablespoons chili powder
1 tablespoon GHIRARDELLI
  GROUND CHOCOLATE
1½ teaspoons garlic salt
1 teaspoon cumin
¼ teaspoon pepper
1 can (16 oz.) kidney beans, drained
½ cup chopped green pepper

In heavy saucepan, sauté bacon until light brown; stir in oil and onion. Add meat and fry until brown. Add tomatoes, chili powder, Ground Chocolate, garlic salt, cumin, and pepper; heat to boiling. Add kidney beans and green pepper. Simmer, covered, 20 minutes. Garnish each bowl with grated Cheddar cheese and chopped green pepper, if desired. Serve with hot corn bread. Makes 4 (1½)servings.

NOTE: Adjust chili powder to give the degree of hotness you prefer.

A different kind of salad using leftover chili . . .

MEXICALI LUNCHEON SALAD

For each salad, make a 1-inch horizontal slice from a head of iceberg lettuce. Place slice on plate; cover with 1 cup hot Western Chili Con Chocolate. Garnish with ½ cup shredded cheddar cheese, 6 avocado slices and ½ cup corn chips. Top with 2 tablespoons crisp fried bacon bits.

Mama mia! What a spaghetti sauce!

NORTH BEACH SPAGHETTI SAUCE

½ pound lean ground beef
2 tablespoons olive oil
1 cup chopped onion
1 cup chopped fresh mushrooms
3 cloves garlic, minced
1 can (28 oz.) Italian-style tomatoes, crushed
1 can (8 oz.) tomato purée
½ cup dry red wine
¼ cup grated Parmesan cheese
2 tablespoons minced parsley
1½ teaspoons GHIRARDELLI GROUND CHOCOLATE
1 teaspoon salt
2 teaspoons Italian herbs
½ teaspoon seasoned salt
¼ teaspoon pepper
1 pound spaghetti

Brown meat in olive oil with onion, mushrooms and garlic. Add remaining ingredients, except spaghetti. Simmer, uncovered, 30 minutes. Cook spaghetti according to package directions. Serve sauce over cooked spaghetti. Sprinkle with additional Parmesan cheese, if desired. Makes 5 cups sauce. Spaghetti with sauce makes 6 servings.

NOTE: This sauce is also great for Lasagna.

Microwave Directions
In 2-quart casserole dish, microwave meat 4 minutes on HIGH. Break up meat; add oil, onion, mushrooms and garlic. Cover and microwave, for 2 minutes on HIGH. Add remaining ingredients, except spaghetti. Cover and microwave on HIGH for 10 minutes; stir. Microwave, uncovered, for 10 minutes, stirring 3 times. Let stand 5 minutes.

Brown your roast with chocolate . . .

BURGUNDY POTTED ROAST

2½ pounds chuck roast
¼ cup flour
1 teaspoon GHIRARDELLI GROUND CHOCOLATE
½ teaspoon seasoned salt
¼ teaspoon pepper
2–3 tablespoons oil
1 can (10 oz.) onion soup with beef stock
½ cup Burgundy wine
¼ cup water
2 cups sliced fresh mushrooms
2 slices lemon
½ teaspoon fine herbs
¼ teaspoon caraway seeds

Dredge meat in mixture of flour, Ground Chocolate, seasoned salt and pepper. Use all of flour mixture. In heavy pan, brown meat in hot oil. Add remaining ingredients. Simmer, covered, 2 hours or until meat is tender. Serve with buttered twisted egg noodles sprinkled with dill weed. Makes 6 servings.

A square meal with a touch of San Francisco Chocolate . . .

MISSION DOLORES BEEF STEW

2 pounds beef chuck, cut into 2-inch cubes
¼ cup flour
1 teaspoon seasoned salt
¼ teaspoon pepper
2–3 tablespoons oil
1 can (14 oz.) beef broth
½ cup dry red wine
1 bay leaf
1 tablespoon GHIRARDELLI GROUND CHOCOLATE
½ teaspoon dry mustard
½ teaspoon chili powder
¼ teaspoon oregano
1 clove garlic, minced
7 small whole onions
2 whole cloves
2 cups quartered potatoes
2 cups carrot pieces
2 cups quartered fresh mushrooms
¼ cup chopped parsley

Dredge meat in mixture of flour, seasoned salt and pepper. In Dutch oven, brown meat in hot oil. Add beef broth, wine, bay leaf, Ground Chocolate, mustard, chili powder, oregano, garlic and one onion, cut up. Heat to boiling; simmer, covered, 2 hours. Stick cloves into 2 onions and add remaining vegetables to stew; simmer, covered, 45 minutes. Stir in parsley. Makes 6 (1½ cups) servings.

Dress up the birds with chocolate orange glaze . . .

NOB HILL GRAND CORNISH GAME HENS

4 Cornish game hens, thawed
1 medium onion, quartered
⅓ cup Grand Marnier liqueur
1 tablespoon GHIRARDELLI
    GROUND CHOCOLATE
1 tablespoon butter
Pinch salt
Parsley sprigs

Season hens, inside and out, with salt and pepper. Place 1 onion quarter into each cavity. To prepare sauce, combine Grand Marnier with Ground Chocolate, butter and salt. Pour 1 teaspoon sauce in each cavity. Brush sauce over skin of hens. Place hens, breast side down, on baking pan with rack. Bake at 350° F for 30 minutes. Turn breast side up and brush with sauce. Bake additional 30 minutes, brushing twice with remaining sauce. Place hens on serving plate. Drain drippings from pan; pour over hens. Stuff a small bunch parsley into cavity of each hen. Flame with additional Grand Marnier, if desired. Serve with wild rice and spiced peaches. Makes 4 servings.

Microwave Directions
A good microwave recipe, because the Ground Chocolate allows the hens to color brown. Prepare hens and sauce as directed above. Arrange hens, breast side down, in 9 by 13-inch baking dish. Cover with waxed paper. Microwave on HIGH 15 minutes. Turn hens and baste. Shield legs with small pieces of foil. Microwave, uncovered, on HIGH for 10 minutes or until tender. Cover and let stand 5 minutes.

The clue of perfect meat loaf . . .

BAKER STREET MEAT LOAF

2 pounds lean ground beef
1 teaspoon salt
½ teaspoon pepper
1 tablespoon GHIRARDELLI
   GROUND CHOCOLATE
½ teaspoon poultry seasoning
½ cup finely chopped celery
1 can (10½ oz.) onion soup with beef
   stock
2 eggs, beaten
½ cup dry bread crumbs

Combine all ingredients. Press into 9 by 5-inch loaf pan. Bake at 350° F for one hour. Makes 8 servings.

MUSHROOM GRAVY

Drippings from Baker Street Meat
   Loaf (recipe above)
2 tablespoons flour
1 cup milk
½ teaspoon GHIRARDELLI GROUND
   CHOCOLATE
1 can (2½ oz.) sliced mushrooms

In saucepan, combine drippings and flour, blending with wire whip. Add milk, Ground Chocolate and mushrooms. Heat to boiling; simmer 5 minutes. Season with salt and pepper. Makes 2 cups gravy.

Touch of San Francisco chocolate complements Far East recipe . . .

SAN FRANCISCO CHICKEN CURRY

3 pounds frying chicken parts
3 cups water
1 teaspoon seasoned salt
¾ cup minced onion
1 clove garlic, minced
¾ cup chopped tart apple
6 tablespoons butter
1–2 tablespoons curry powder
¼ teaspoon dry mustard
¼ teaspoon ginger
¼ teaspoon ground cardamom
Dash nutmeg
1 teaspoon salt
¼ teaspoon pepper
1 tablespoon GHIRARDELLI
   GROUND CHOCOLATE
¼ cup flour
1 tablespoon lemon juice

Cook chicken with water and seasoned salt, covered, for 1 hour. Reserve stock; debone chicken and cut up meat. Sauté onion, garlic and apple in butter. Stir in curry, mustard, ginger, cardamom, nutmeg, salt, pepper, Ground Chocolate and flour; simmer 5 minutes. Add lemon juice and two cups chicken stock. On low heat, stir until sauce thickens. Add chicken meat; simmer, covered, 20 minutes. Add stock as needed to thin. Serve curry over rice. Select a combination of condiments: Chutney, chopped peanuts or almonds, toasted coconut, raisins soaked in wine, diced banana, chopped cucumber or chopped green pepper. Makes 6 (¾ cup) servings.

Spicy Mexican chicken with California chocolate . . .

CALIFORNIA-STYLE CHICKEN MOLÉ

3 pounds frying chicken parts
½ cup butter or margarine
1½ cups water
1 cup chopped onion
2 cloves garlic, minced
1 can (4 oz.) diced green chiles
½ cup sliced almonds
1 tablespoon sesame seeds
1 teaspoon salt
½ teaspoon chili powder
½ teaspoon cumin
¼ teaspoon anise seed
¼ teaspoon cilantro (coriander leaf)
¼ teaspoon chervil
¼ teaspoon pepper
¼ teaspoon cinnamon
Pinch ground cloves
2 sections (1 oz.) GHIRARDELLI SEMI-SWEET CHOCOLATE
2 tablespoons corn meal
½ cup fresh diced tomatoes

Brown chicken in ¼ cup butter. Sprinkle with salt and pepper. Add water and simmer, covered, 1 hour. Drain and reserve stock. Sauté onion and garlic in ¼ cup butter. In blender, combine onion, green chiles, nuts, sesame seeds, salt and spices. Blend until smooth. In saucepan, combine blended mixture, broken chocolate and corn meal. Cook until sauce is thick. Stir in tomatoes. Simmer 15 minutes. Pour sauce over chicken; simmer 10 minutes. Serve in colorful Mexican casserole dish. Makes 6 servings.

Spicy cherry sauce adds glamour to baked ham . . .

RED BRICK BAKED HAM WITH CHERRY SAUCE

5–7 pound ham
Whole cloves
1 can (17 oz.) dark pitted cherries in
 syrup
½ cup sweet vermouth
1½ tablespoon cornstarch
1 teaspoon GHIRARDELLI GROUND
 CHOCOLATE
Pinch ground cloves
⅛ teaspoon ginger

Score fat surface of ham in 1-inch squares. Stud with whole cloves. Bake ham at 350° F for about 2 hours. (Bake canned ham at 325° F.) In saucepan, combine remaining ingredients; heat to boiling and cook until thickened. Baste ham with Cherry Sauce last 15 minutes of baking. Slice ham and serve with remaining Cherry Sauce. Makes 1¾ cups sauce.

NOTE: Cherry Sauce is also delicious served with roast duckling or baked chicken breasts.

CHERRIES JUBILEE DESSERT

Follow recipe above for Cherry Sauce, using 1 tablespoon Ground Chocolate and omit ground cloves. Serve warm Cherry Sauce over vanilla ice cream.

Chocolate, the secret ingredient in this special barbecue sauce . . .

POLK GULCH SPARERIBS

3½ pounds pork spareribs
1 cup tomato catsup
1 cup onion pieces
1 clove garlic
1 tablespoon GHIRARDELLI
   GROUND CHOCOLATE
1 tablespoon liquid smoke
1 tablespoon lemon juice
1 tablespoon honey
½ teaspoon ginger
Pinch pepper

Sprinkle spareribs with salt and pepper. Place fat side down on rack in shallow broiler pan. Bake at 400° F for 30 minutes. In blender, combine remaining ingredients and mix until smooth. In saucepan, heat to boiling; cook, covered, 10 minutes. Sauce may be thinned with water, if desired. Baste spareribs with sauce. Lower heat to 325° F and continue baking for one hour or until done. During baking time, turn and baste spareribs with remaining sauce. Cut between bones. Makes 4 servings.

OVEN BARBECUE CHICKEN

Prepare barbecue sauce as directed in recipe for Polk Gulch Spareribs. Marinate 3 pounds cut up chicken in barbecue sauce for 1 hour or overnight. Bake, uncovered, at 375° F for 1 hour. Makes 4–6 servings.

Touch of chocolate makes lamb dinner a royal treat . . .

EMPEROR NORTON LEG OF LAMB

5–6 pound leg of lamb
2 tablespoons chopped onion
1 large clove garlic, pressed
½ cup Marsala wine
1 tablespoon GHIRARDELLI
   GROUND CHOCOLATE
1 tablespoon chopped fresh mint
1 tablespoon oil
1 teaspoon grated lemon rind
¼ teaspoon seasoned salt
¼ teaspoon fine herbs
Pinch pepper

Place lamb on rack in roasting pan. Press onion and garlic in a garlic press. Combine with remaining ingredients for basting sauce. Brush sauce over lamb; sprinkle with salt and pepper. Roast lamb at 400° F for 30 minutes. Lower heat to 325° F. Turn and baste lamb every 30 minutes for the next two hours. For rare lamb, bake less time, testing with meat thermometer. Remove lamb to serving platter. Serve with chilled pear halves marinated in green crème de menthe. Makes 6–8 servings.

EMPEROR NORTON GRAVY

Deglaze roasting pan with 1½ cups boiling water; pour into saucepan. Blend 3 tablespoons flour with ¼ cup Marsala wine; add to liquid. Stir with wire whip, cooking until thick and smooth. Season with salt and pepper.

RACK OF LAMB

A rack of lamb is so easy to prepare and always impresses guests. Allow 2 chops per person and order accordingly from your butcher. The largest rack is 8 ribs. Baste with half the recipe for the basting sauce used in Emperor Norton Leg of Lamb recipe (page 64). Roast at 350° F for approximately one hour.

Even vegetables like chocolate . . .

CARROTS AND ONIONS ROYALE

¼ cup butter
2 tablespoons honey
1 tablespoon GHIRARDELLI GROUND CHOCOLATE
¼ teaspoon salt
Dash white pepper
1 can (16 oz.) tiny whole carrots
1 can (16 oz.) tiny whole onions

In saucepan, combine butter, honey, Ground Chocolate, salt, pepper and 1 tablespoon liquid drained from carrots; heat to boiling. Arrange drained carrots and onions in casserole dish. Pour heated sauce over vegetables. Bake at 350° F for 25 minutes, stirring once. Makes 5 servings.

NOTE: Two cups fresh carrot chunks and two cups fresh boiling onions may be substituted for canned vegetables. Peel and precook in salted water.

GHIRARDELLI'S

GROUND CHOCOLATE

Say "Gear-ar-delly"

fills every cocoa and chocolate need!

PIES and CAKES

Easy to make in a food processor . . .

CHOCOLATE LOVERS' CHEESE PIE

2 packages (8 oz. each) cream
   cheese, softened
½ cup sugar
3 eggs
1 package (4 oz.) GHIRARDELLI
   SEMI-SWEET CHOCOLATE
8-inch prepared chocolate or graham
   cracker pie shell
1 cup sour cream
½ cup powdered sugar
½ teaspoon vanilla

In a food processor or mixer, beat cream cheese with sugar; add eggs. Melt chocolate in double boiler or in microwave oven on MEDIUM for 2–3 minutes. Add melted chocolate to cream cheese mixture, beating until thick and smooth. Spread into pie shell. Bake at 350°F for 30–35 minutes or until firm in center. Cool. Blend sour cream with powdered sugar and vanilla. Spread over cheese pie. Bake additional 5 minutes. Chill 4 hours or overnight. Decorate top with chocolate curls, if desired. Makes 8 servings.

An "earthy" pie with a touch of class . . .

MOTHER LODE APPLE PIE

Filling
- 4 cups peeled, thickly sliced tart apples
- 1 tablespoon lemon juice
- ¾ cup sugar
- 3 tablespoons GHIRARDELLI GROUND CHOCOLATE
- 1 tablespoon cornstarch
- ½ teaspoon cinnamon
- ¼ teaspoon nutmeg
- Pinch allspice
- ⅛ teaspoon salt
- 2 tablespoons cold butter or margarine
- 9-inch unbaked pie shell

Filling

Toss apples with lemon juice. Blend sugar with Ground Chocolate, cornstarch, spices and salt; mix with apples. Cut butter into small cubes; toss with apples. Pile apples in pie shell.

Topping
- ½ cup flour
- 1 tablespoon sugar
- 2 tablespoons packed brown sugar
- ⅛ teaspoon salt
- ¼ cup butter or margarine, softened
- ¼ cup chopped pecans

Topping

Mix flour with sugar, brown sugar and salt. With pastry blender, work in butter; add nuts. Sprinkle topping over apples. Place on baking sheet. Bake at 450°F for 10 minutes. Lower heat to 350°F and bake additional 30 minutes. Serve at room temperature or slightly warm. Makes 6 servings.

An old-fashioned dessert that still has glamour . . .

VICTORIAN BLACK BOTTOM PIE

9-inch baked pie shell

Chocolate Filling
¼ cup sugar
2½ tablespoons cornstarch
⅛ teaspoon salt
1⅓ cups milk
1 tablespoon dark rum
1 bar (4 oz.) GHIRARDELLI
   SEMI-SWEET CHOCOLATE

Cream Filling
1 package (3⅛ oz.) vanilla pudding
   mix
1 cup milk
½ cup half and half
¼ cup light rum
1 tablespoon butter

Topping
½ pint whipping cream
2 tablespoons powdered sugar
1 teaspoon vanilla

Chocolate Filling
In heavy saucepan, blend sugar with cornstarch and salt. Mix in milk and rum. Add 7 sections broken chocolate. (Reserve 1 section for Topping.) With wire whip, stir constantly until chocolate melts and mixture comes to hard boil. Pour into pie shell. Cover surface with plastic wrap to prevent film. Chill while preparing Cream Filling.

Cream Filling
In heavy saucepan, combine pudding mix, milk, half and half, rum and butter. Stir constantly over low heat until mixture comes to hard boil. Cool 5 minutes. Stir and spoon over Chocolate Filling. Cover surface with plastic wrap. Chill 2 hours or until firm.

Topping
Whip cream with powdered sugar and vanilla until stiff. Grate remaining section chocolate. Fold grated chocolate into whipped cream. Spread over pie. Chill. Makes 6 servings.

Refrigerated or frozen, it's delicious! . . .
Can be prepared a day in advance.

SAN FRANCISCO MINT CHOCOLATE PIE

½ cup milk
3⅓ cups miniature marshmallows
   (22 large)
½ of 12 oz. package (1 cup)
   FLICK-ETTE MINT CHOCOLATE
   FLAVOR CHIPS
½ pint whipping cream
8-inch prepared graham cracker pie
   shell

In heavy saucepan, heat milk with marshmallows, stirring until smooth. Add Flick-ettes, stirring until melted. Chill 15 minutes. Whip cream until almost stiff. Fold into chilled mixture. Pour into pie shell. Chill 2 hours or overnight in refrigerator or freezer. Garnish with additional whipped cream and shaved chocolate, if desired. Makes 6–8 servings.

Down South goodness in foggy San Francisco . . .

CLIFF HOUSE CHOCOLATE PECAN PIE

1 bar (4 oz.) GHIRARDELLI
   SEMI-SWEET CHOCOLATE
2 tablespoons butter or margarine
⅔ cup light corn syrup
3 eggs
1 tablespoon vanilla
¼ teaspoon salt
⅔ cup sugar
1 cup pecans (chopped or halves)
9-inch unbaked pie shell

In double boiler, melt chocolate with butter over 1-inch simmering water; stir in corn syrup. Beat eggs slightly with vanilla and salt; stir in sugar, chocolate mixture and nuts. Pour into pie shell. Bake at 400°F for 15 minutes. Reduce heat to 350°F and continue baking 30 minutes; cool. Serve with whipped cream, if desired. Makes 6 servings.

THE chocolate pie for chocolate lovers . . .

HEAVENLY CHOCOLATE PIE

2 cups milk
4 tablespoons butter
¾ cup GHIRARDELLI GROUND
  CHOCOLATE
¼ cup sugar
¼ cup cornstarch
Pinch salt
3 egg yolks
1 teaspoon vanilla
9-inch baked pie shell

In double boiler, scald milk with butter. Blend Ground Chocolate with sugar, cornstarch and salt. Using a wire whip, beat chocolate mixture into hot milk. Stir constantly for 5 minutes, or until filling begins to thicken. Mix a small amount of hot filling with egg yolks, then pour yolks into filling. Continue cooking a few minutes, stirring, until thick enough to hold a shape. Add vanilla. Pour into baked pie shell. Cover with plastic wrap touching surface to prevent film. Top with meringue or whipped cream. Makes 6 servings.

72

GOLDEN GATE BANANA SPLIT PIE

1 quart vanilla ice cream
1 package (6 oz.) GHIRARDELLI
  SEMI-SWEET CHOCOLATE CHIPS
9-inch baked pie shell
1 pint strawberry ice cream
1 banana
Whipping cream, whipped
Chopped nuts
Cherry halves

To make Chocolate Sauce, melt 1 cup vanilla ice cream in double boiler. Add Chocolate Chips, stirring until melted. Cool sauce. Fill baked pie shell with remaining vanilla ice cream, alternating with strawberry ice cream. Put in freezer until serving time. Just before serving, pour Chocolate Sauce over ice cream. Decorate with banana slices, whipped cream, nuts and cherries. Serve immediately. Makes 8 servings.

Chocolate crumb crust complements this minty pie . . .

BUENA VISTA GRASSHOPPER PIE

Crumb Crust
¼ cup melted butter
1¼ cups graham cracker crumbs
¼ cup GHIRARDELLI GROUND CHOCOLATE
4 tablespoons sugar

Filling
2 packages (3 oz. each) lime flavored gelatin
1½ cups boiling water
⅓ cup green crème de menthe
⅓ cup white crème de cacao
1 pint vanilla ice cream, softened
½ pint whipping cream
2 tablespoons powdered sugar
2 bars (1⅛ oz. each) GHIRARDELLI MINT CHOCOLATE

Crust
Mix butter with crumbs, Ground Chocolate and sugar. Press into 9-inch pie plate. Bake at 350°F for 6 minutes. Cool.

Filling
Dissolve gelatin in boiling water. Add crème de menthe and crème de cacao. Stir in softened ice cream. Chill 5–10 minutes until slightly thickened. Pour into crumb crust. Chill until firm. Whip cream with powdered sugar. Grate 1 mint bar; stir into whipped cream. Spread over pie filling. Decorate top with chocolate curls made from the remaining mint bar. Makes 8 servings.

73

In the West, we say Sacramento River Mud Pie . . .

MISSISSIPPI MUD PIE

1 bar (4 oz.) GHIRARDELLI SWEET
   CHOCOLATE
½ cup butter
3 eggs
3 tablespoons light corn syrup
1 cup sugar
1 teaspoon vanilla
Pinch salt
9-inch unbaked deep pastry pie shell
1 pint vanilla ice cream

In heavy saucepan or microwave oven, melt chocolate with butter. Beat eggs; mix in syrup, sugar and vanilla. Combine with chocolate mixture. Pour into unbaked pie shell. Bake at 350°F for 35–40 minutes or until top is cracked and filling is still soft. Cool to room temperature. Top each wedge with scoop of ice cream. Makes 8 servings.

74

You will never forget Ghirardelli Square . . .

GHIRARDELLI SQUARE CAKE

1 cup butter or margarine, softened
½ cup sugar
½ cup packed brown sugar
2 eggs, well beaten
2 teaspoons vanilla
2½ cups sifted cake flour
1½ cups GHIRARDELLI GROUND
   CHOCOLATE
½ teaspoon salt
1 teaspoon baking powder
1 teaspoon baking soda
1 cup milk

Cream butter with sugar and brown sugar until fluffy; beat in eggs and vanilla. Sift flour with Ground Chocolate, salt, baking powder and soda. Add dry ingredients alternately with milk, ending with dry ingredients. Grease bottoms of 2 (8-inch square) cake pans or 2 (9-inch round) cake pans. Line with waxed paper. Spread batter into cake pans. Bake at 350°F for 30–35 minutes. Cool on racks 10–15 minutes; remove from pans. Frost with Pink Brick Frosting.

PINK BRICK FROSTING

2 egg whites
1½ cups sugar
⅛ teaspoon salt
⅓ cup cold water
2 teaspoons light corn syrup
2 teaspoons vanilla
Few drops red food coloring

Combine all ingredients in double boiler over 1-inch simmering water. Beat with electric mixer 7–8 minutes until frosting forms peaks. Spread frosting on Ghirardelli Square Cake. Sprinkle with crushed peppermint sticks, if desired.

Grandma's favorite recipe with avant-garde flair . . .

REDWOOD GINGERBREAD

3 eggs
¾ cup sugar
1 cup oil
1 cup molasses
3 cups flour
¾ cup GHIRARDELLI GROUND
   CHOCOLATE
2 teaspoons baking soda
1 teaspoon baking powder
1 teaspoon salt
1½ teaspoons ginger
1 teaspoon cinnamon
½ teaspoon nutmeg
⅛ teaspoon ground cloves
1 cup buttermilk

Beat eggs with sugar; mix in oil and molasses. Sift flour with Ground Chocolate, baking soda, baking powder, salt and spices. Add dry ingredients alternately with buttermilk, beating well after each addition. Spread batter into greased 9 by 13-inch pan. Bake 350°F for 40–45 minutes. Cool. Cut into squares. Serve with Chocolate Whipped Cream (page 124), if desired. Makes 24 (2-inch) squares.

Favorite San Francisco loaf cake with spicy chocolate flavor . . .

GOLD DIGGER'S CHOCOLATE SPICE CAKE

1 cup GHIRARDELLI GROUND
   CHOCOLATE
1½ cups flour
1 cup sugar
1½ teaspoons pumpkin pie spice
1½ teaspoons baking powder
½ teaspoon salt
½ cup butter or margarine, softened
¾ cup milk
1½ teaspoons vanilla
2 eggs

Into mixer bowl, sift together Ground Chocolate, flour, sugar, spice, baking powder and salt. Make a well in center; add butter, milk and vanilla. Mix to blend, then beat 5 minutes on high speed of mixer. Add eggs, one at a time, beating well after each addition. Pour into greased 9 by 5-inch loaf pan. Bake at 350°F 1 hour or until baked in center. Cool 15 minutes; remove from pan. Serve plain or frosted.

MILK CHOCOLATE FROSTING

1 package (10 oz.) GHIRARDELLI
   MILK CHOCOLATE BLOCKS
1 teaspoon butter
¼ cup milk
Dash salt
1 teaspoon vanilla

In double boiler, melt chocolate with butter over 1-inch simmering water, stirring constantly. Stir in milk and salt. Remove from heat. Add vanilla and beat until thick and smooth. Makes enough frosting for 9 by 13-inch cake or 14 cupcakes.

Always a success for party or lunch pail . . .

BONANZA KING DEVIL'S FOOD CAKE

2 cups sifted cake flour
1½ cups GHIRARDELLI GROUND
   CHOCOLATE
1 cup sugar
2 teaspoons baking soda
½ teaspoon cream of tartar
½ teaspoon salt
1 cup shortening
1½ cups buttermilk
3 eggs
1½ teaspoons vanilla

Into a mixer bowl, sift flour with Ground Chocolate, sugar, baking soda, cream of tartar and salt. Add shortening and 1 cup buttermilk. Beat on medium speed for 2 minutes. Scrape down bowl. Add ½ cup buttermilk, eggs and vanilla. Beat additional 2 minutes on medium speed. Grease bottoms of 2 (9 by 1½-inch round) cake pans. Line with waxed paper. Spread batter into pans. Bake at 350°F for 30–35 minutes. Cool on racks 10–15 minutes; remove from pans.

STRIKE-IT-RICH CHOCOLATE BUTTER CREAM FROSTING

1 bar (4 oz.) GHIRARDELLI SEMI-
   SWEET CHOCOLATE
¼ cup water
¼ teaspoon instant coffee (optional)
2½ cups sifted powdered sugar
2 egg yolks
½ teaspoon vanilla
6 tablespoons butter (very soft)

In medium-sized heavy saucepan, melt broken chocolate with water and coffee. Stir constantly until mixture is very smooth. Remove from heat. Mix in sugar and beat until smooth. Beat in egg yolks and vanilla. Place pan in bowl of ice and water. Add butter, in four additions, beating until frosting is very light in color and thick enough to spread. Frost Bonanza King Devil's Food Cake or other favorite chocolate cake. Chill to set frosting.

Tunnel of lovely chocolate . . .

CHOCOLATE BARON BUNDT CAKE

1 package (18½ oz.) chocolate cake
  mix with pudding
4 eggs
1 cup sour cream
½ cup oil
1 teaspoon vanilla
1 cup finely chopped walnuts
1 package (12 oz.) FLICK-ETTE
  MINT CHOCOLATE FLAVORED
  CHIPS

In mixer bowl, combine cake mix, eggs, sour cream, oil
and vanilla; Beat at medium speed for 4 minutes. Fold
in nuts. Pour half of batter into well greased 10-inch
bundt pan. Sprinkle with 1 cup Flick-ettes. Cover with
remaining batter. Bake at 350°F for 50–55 minutes or
until cake springs back in center when touched lightly.
Cool in pan on cake rack for 20 minutes. Gently
remove cake from pan. Makes 12 servings.

Chocolate Glaze
Melt remaining 1 cup Flick-ettes with ¼ cup water.
Cool 20 minutes to thicken. Spoon glaze over top of
cake and drizzle down sides. Cake may be served
slightly warm with soft glaze.

As dark and moist as a walk through the woods . . .

MUIR WOODS CHOCOLATE CHERRY CAKE

1 package (6 oz.) GHIRARDELLI
   SEMI-SWEET CHOCOLATE CHIPS
¼ cup water
¾ cup butter or margarine, softened
1¾ cups sugar
1½ teaspoons vanilla
3 eggs
2¼ cups unsifted cake flour
1 teaspoon baking powder
1 teaspoon baking soda
½ teaspoon salt
1 cup buttermilk

In heavy saucepan, melt Chocolate Chips with water, stirring constantly; cool. Cream butter, gradually adding sugar and vanilla. Add eggs, one at a time, beating well after each addition. Blend in chocolate. Sift flour with baking powder, baking soda and salt. Add dry ingredients alternately with buttermilk, beating until blended. Spread batter into 3 waxed paper-lined 9-inch round cake pans. Bake at 375°F for about 25 minutes. Cool on rack for 10 minutes. Remove cake and waxed paper; cool. Fill with Muir Woods Cherry Cream Filling (recipe below). Frost top and sides with Chocolate Sour Cream Frosting (page 81). Makes 12 servings.

MUIR WOODS CHERRY CREAM FILLING

1 can (1 lb.) sour pitted cherries,
   drained
2 tablespoons sugar
¼ cup Kirsch (cherry liqueur)
1 teaspoon unflavored gelatin
½ pint whipping cream
3 tablespoons powdered sugar

Marinate cherries with sugar and Kirsch for at least 2 hours. Drain liquid; add a tablespoon to gelatin. Melt gelatin over hot water; add remaining Kirsch liquid. Whip cream until thick. Slowly add gelatin mixture and powdered sugar. Beat until stiff. Combine with cherries. Spread as filling between layers of Muir Woods Chocolate Cherry Cake. Chill to firm filling.

80

CHOCOLATE SOUR CREAM FROSTING FOR CHERRY CAKE

½ cup sour cream
1 teaspoon vanilla
2 cups powdered sugar
1 package (6 oz.) GHIRARDELLI
 SEMI-SWEET CHOCOLATE CHIPS

Beat sour cream and vanilla with powdered sugar until creamy. In double boiler, melt Chocolate Chips over 1-inch simmering water. Mix chocolate into sour cream mixture, whipping until smooth and thick. Frost top and sides of Muir Woods Chocolate Cherry Cake. Decorate top with stemmed cherries marinated in Kirsch, if desired.

DOMINGO'S CHOCOLATE FROSTING

½ of 4 oz. bar (4 sections)
 GHIRARDELLI SEMI-SWEET
 CHOCOLATE
3 tablespoons butter or margarine
3 tablespoons milk
⅛ teaspoon salt
2 cups powdered sugar
½ teaspoon vanilla

In heavy saucepan, melt broken chocolate with butter, milk and salt. Sift powdered sugar into bowl. Add chocolate and beat thoroughly. Add vanilla and beat until thick. Spread over your favorite chocolate cake.

The everlasting favorite cake . . .

GOLD RUSH CARROT CAKE

1½ cups oil
1⅔ cups sugar
4 eggs
2 cups flour
⅓ cup GHIRARDELLI GROUND
   CHOCOLATE
2 teaspoons baking soda
2 teaspoons cinnamon
1 teaspoon salt
3 cups shredded carrots (packed)
¾ cup finely chopped walnuts

Mix oil with sugar; add eggs one at a time, beating well after each addition. Sift flour with Ground Chocolate, baking soda, cinnamon and salt. Add dry ingredients to creamed mixture. Mix in carrots and nuts. Greese bottom of 9 by 13-inch cake pan. Spread batter into pan. Bake at 350°F for 45–50 minutes. Cool 30 minutes. Spread White Chocolate Frosting on warm cake. Sprinkle with additional chopped nuts, if desired.

CHOCOLATE ZUCCHINI CAKE

Prepare Gold Rush Carrot Cake, substituting 3 cups shredded zucchini (packed) for carrots.

WHITE CHOCOLATE FROSTING

3 cups powdered sugar, sifted
1 package (3 oz.) cream cheese,
  softened
3 tablespoons half and half
2 teaspoons vanilla
⅛ teaspoon salt
4 oz. sweet white chocolate
2 tablespoons butter

In mixer, blend sifted powdered sugar, cream cheese, half and half, vanilla and salt. In double boiler, melt white chocolate with butter over 1-inch simmering water. Add to creamed mixture. Beat until smooth. Spread on Gold Rush Carrot Cake.

CHOCOLATE CREAM CHEESE FROSTING

Prepare White Chocolate Frosting, substituting 4 oz. bar Ghirardelli Semi-Sweet Chocolate for white chocolate in recipe.

Chocolate, the universal language . . .

ONE LAYER CHOCOLATE SOUR CREAM CAKE

½ of 4 oz. bar (4 sections)
  GHIRARDELLI SEMI-SWEET
  CHOCOLATE
¼ cup water
⅓ cup butter
⅓ cup sugar
⅓ cup packed brown sugar
1 teaspoon vanilla
1 egg plus 1 egg yolk, beaten
½ cup sour cream
1 cup unsifted cake flour
¾ teaspoon baking powder
½ teaspoon baking soda
¼ teaspoon salt

In heavy saucepan, melt chocolate with water over low heat, stirring constantly. Cream butter with sugar and brown sugar; add vanilla and eggs, beating until fluffy. Mix in sour cream. Sift flour with baking powder, baking soda and salt. Add dry ingredients alternately with chocolate liquid, mixing well after each addition. Spread batter into waxed paper-lined 9-inch round cake pan. Bake at 350° F for 30 minutes. Cool on rack for 10–15 minutes. Remove cake and waxed paper. Makes one layer.

MT. SHASTA BAKED ALASKA

One Layer Chocolate Sour Cream
    Cake (page 84)
1 pint ice cream, any flavor
½ cup egg whites
¼ teaspoon cream of tartar
⅛ teaspoon salt
1 teaspoon vanilla
½ cup sugar

To assemble dessert, spread slightly softened ice cream over cake, leaving 1-inch margin around edge. For color contrast, 2 flavors of ice cream may be combined. Place in freezer until ready to serve. Beat egg whites until foamy; add cream of tartar, salt and vanilla. On high speed, beat until soft peaks form. Add sugar gradually, beating until stiff peaks form. Spread meringue over ice cream and cake. Sprinkle with sliced almonds, if desired. Place dessert on piece of heavy brown paper on baking sheet. Bake at 450°F for 5 minutes. Serve immediately with Chocolate Zabaglione Sauce (page 124). Makes 8 servings.

OCCIDENTAL CHOCOLATE RUM RING

3 cups unsifted flour
2 cups GHIRARDELLI GROUND
    CHOCOLATE
2 cups sugar
1 tablespoon baking powder
1 teaspoon salt
1 cup butter, softened
1½ cups half and half
1 tablespoon vanilla
3 eggs
¼ cup rum

Into large mixer bowl, sift flour with Ground Chocolate, sugar, baking powder and salt. Add butter, half and half and vanilla to center of dry ingredients. Mix together and beat on high speed 5 minutes. Add eggs one at a time, beating well after each addition. Mix in rum. Pour into well-greased 10-inch angel food cake pan. Bake at 325°F for approximately 1½ hours. Slices of cake may be served with vanilla ice cream and chocolate sauce or simply dusted with sifted powdered sugar. Makes 16 servings.

Discover nuggets of pineapple in this roll . . .

FORTY-NINER CHOCOLATE ROLL

4 eggs, separated
1 teaspoon vanilla
½ cup GHIRARDELLI GROUND CHOCOLATE
¼ cup boiling water
¾ cup sifted cake flour
½ teaspoon baking powder
⅛ teaspoon salt
½ cup sugar
½ pint whipping cream
3 tablespoons powdered sugar
1 can (15¼ oz.) crushed pineapple, drained
3 tablespoons rum

Beat egg yolks with vanilla. Blend Ground Chocolate with water; beat into egg yolk mixture. Sift flour with baking powder. Gradually add dry ingredients, mixing until smooth. Beat egg whites with salt until soft peaks form. Gradually add sugar, beating until stiff peaks. Using metal spatula, fold egg whites into chocolate mixture. Pour batter into greased and floured waxed paper-lined 10 by 15-inch jelly roll pan. Bake at 325°F for 15 minutes. Run knife around edge. Turn hot cake onto cloth heavily dusted with powdered sugar. Remove waxed paper, and starting from narrow end, roll up cake with cloth; cool. To make filling, whip cream with powdered sugar until stiff. Stir in pineapple and rum. Unroll cake and spread with filling; reroll cake with filling. Chill until firm. Cut into slices. Makes 10–12 servings.

Christmas Chocolate Log Dessert . . .

BÛCHE DE NOËL

Prepare Forty-Niner Chocolate Roll as directed. Cut 2 slices, 1 inch each, to use for tree knots. Spread cake roll with Strike-It-Rich Chocolate Butter Cream Frosting (page 78). Place the 2 cake slices on top of cake log and frost around them. Use fork to make bark marks on frosting. Arrange a cluster of maraschino cherry halves on log for berries. Decorate plate with Christmas greens and mushroom meringues, if desired.

PARTY CHOCOLATE SPONGE CAKE

6 eggs, separated
2 teaspoons vanilla
1 cup sugar
⅔ cup GHIRARDELLI GROUND CHOCOLATE
½ cup boiling water
1½ cups unsifted cake flour
1 teaspoon baking powder
¼ teaspoon salt.

Beat egg yolks with vanilla; gradually add sugar, beating until light and thick. Mix Ground Chocolate with water; cool. Beat into creamed mixture. Sift flour with baking powder. Gradually add dry ingredients, mixing until smooth. Beat egg whites with salt until stiff peaks form. With metal spatula, carefully fold egg whites into chocolate mixture. Pour batter into ungreased 10-inch tube pan. Bake at 325°F for 50 minutes. Invert pan to cool cake completely. Remove cake from pan by running metal spatula around edge. Cake may be dusted with sifted powdered sugar or frosted with Chocolate Whipped Cream (page 124), if desired. Half of the cake may be frozen and used for Clock Tower Chocolate Trifle (page 141).

Pièce de résistance . . .

TREASURE ISLAND CHOCOLATE CHEESE CAKE

88

Crust
4 tablespoons butter or margarine, melted
1 cup graham cracker crumbs
¼ cup GHIRARDELLI GROUND CHOCOLATE
4 tablespoons sugar
⅛ teaspoon cinnamon

Crust
Combine Crust ingredients, using a food processor, if available. Press into bottom of greased 8-inch springform pan. Bake at 350°F for 6 minutes; cool.

Filling
3 packages (8 oz. each) cream cheese, softened
¾ cup sugar
½ cup GHIRARDELLI GROUND CHOCOLATE
1 tablespoon vanilla
4 eggs

Filling
Beat cream cheese until smooth, gradually adding sugar, Ground Chocolate and vanilla. Add eggs one at a time, mixing until smooth after each addition. (Or mix all ingredients in food processor.) Pour into crust. Bake at 350°F for 40–45 minutes; cool completely.

Topping
1 cup sour cream
2 tablespoons GHIRARDELLI GROUND CHOCOLATE
¼ cup sugar

Topping
Whip sour cream with Ground Chocolate and sugar. Spread over cool cheese cake. Bake at 350°F for 5 minutes. Chill several hours or overnight. Makes 12 servings.

As unique as the City itself . . .

ST. FRANCIS DARK FRUIT CAKE

1 pound (3 cups) chopped mixed
   candied fruit
1 cup whole candied cherries
1 cup golden raisins
1 cup sweet sherry wine
1 cup butter, softened
1 cup packed brown sugar
5 eggs
1 cup pecan halves
1 cup slivered almonds
2⅓ cups unsifted flour
1 cup GHIRARDELLI GROUND
   CHOCOLATE
1 teaspoon baking powder
1 teaspoon salt
2 teaspoons cinnamon
1 teaspoon allspice
½ teaspoon nutmeg
½ teaspoon ground cloves
2–4 tablespoons light corn syrup

Soak mixed fruit, cherries and raisins in sherry overnight. Cream butter, gradually adding brown sugar. Beat in eggs, one at a time. Stir in fruit and sherry mixture, pecans and almonds. Sift flour with Ground Chocolate, baking powder, salt and spices. Gradually stir dry ingredients into fruit mixture.

Line 2 (9 by 5-inch) loaf pans with lightly greased waxed paper. Divide batter into prepared pans. For miniature fruit cakes, fill greased muffin cups about ⅔ full. Decorate tops with additional candied cherry halves and nuts, as desired. Bake at 275°F for about 2 hours for loaves and 1 hour for individual cakes or until dry when tested with a toothpick. For surface glaze, brush with corn syrup immediately after removing from oven. Cool cakes on wire rack. Remove from pans. Wrap fruit cakes in cloth dampened with additional sherry. Overwrap with foil or place in tight metal container. Fruit cakes should age 1–4 weeks for mellow flavor. For best results, chill cakes before slicing. Makes 4½ pounds fruit cake.

Beautiful ending to a gourmet dinner . . .

MILLIONAIRE CHOCOLATE TRUFFLE CAKE

1 package (12 oz.) GHIRARDELLI
   SEMI-SWEET CHOCOLATE CHIPS
6 tablespoons butter
2 tablespoons sugar
2 teaspoons flour
1 teaspoon hot water
2 teaspoons vanilla
3 eggs, separated
Pinch salt

Topping
1 package (3 oz.) cream cheese,
   softened
½ pint whipping cream
3 tablespoons powdered sugar
½ teaspoon vanilla

In double boiler, melt Chocolate Chips with butter over 1-inch simmering water. Mix in sugar, flour, water and vanilla. Remove from heat and stir in egg yolks one at a time; cool. Beat egg whites with salt until stiff but not dry. Fold into chocolate mixture. Spread into buttered 8-inch springform pan. Bake at 425°F for 15 minutes. The cake will be soft in the center. Cool.
Makes 12 servings.

Topping
Beat cream cheese until smooth. Gradually add whipping cream, sugar and vanilla. Whip until thick enough to spread over top of cake. Chill several hours.

90

MIDNIGHT CHOCOLATE GLAZE

1 package (6 oz.) GHIRARDELLI
  SEMI-SWEET CHOCOLATE CHIPS
¼ cup hot, strong coffee
1 tablespoon brandy
3 tablespoons butter

In heavy saucepan, melt Chocolate Chips with coffee, or microwave 2–3 minutes on MEDIUM, stirring until very smooth. Add brandy. Mix in butter, a tablespoon at a time, stirring until smooth. Spread over Millionaire Chocolate Truffle Cake or other rich chocolate cake.

AUNT LOTTIE'S POUND CAKE

1 bar (4 oz.) GHIRARDELLI
  SEMI-SWEET CHOCOLATE
1 cup butter, softened
1 cup sugar
5 eggs
1 teaspoon vanilla
1⅓ cups sifted flour
½ teaspoon baking powder

In double boiler, melt chocolate over 1-inch simmering water. Cream butter until light. Gradually add sugar, creaming until fluffy. Add eggs one at a time, beating well after each addition. Blend in vanilla and melted chocolate. Sift flour with baking powder. Gradually mix in dry ingredients. Pour into greased 9 by 5-inch loaf pan. Bake at 350°F for 50–60 minutes.

A tall cake to be enjoyed by a crowd of friends . . .

TELEGRAPH HILL CHOCOLATE CAKE

1 cup milk
2 tablespoons red wine vinegar
1 bar (4 oz.) GHIRARDELLI UNSWEETENED BAKING CHOCOLATE

1 cup shortening
2 cups sugar
2 teaspoons vanilla
5 eggs
2 cups sifted cake flour
1 teaspoon baking soda
½ teaspoon salt

Combine milk with vinegar; let stand to thicken. Melt chocolate according to package directions. Cream shortening with sugar and vanilla. Add eggs one at a time, beating well after each addition. Mix in melted chocolate. Sift flour with baking soda and salt. Add dry ingredients alternately with milk, mixing well after each addition. Line 3 (9 by 1½-inch round) cake pans with waxed paper. Divide batter into pans. Bake at 350°F for 25–30 minutes. Cool on racks 10 minutes. Run knife around edge of pan. Remove cake from pans; peel off waxed paper. Cool on racks. Spread layers with Velvet Coffee Cream Filling. Frost top and sides with Princess Chocolate Frosting. Makes 16 large servings.

VELVET COFFEE CREAM FILLING

1 package (3 oz.) cream cheese,
   softened
⅓ cup powdered sugar
2 tablespoons coffee liqueur
½ pint whipping cream

Beat cream cheese with sugar and liqueur. Gradually add whipping cream, beating until thick enough to hold a shape. Spread between layers of Telegraph Hill Chocolate Cake.

PRINCESS CHOCOLATE FROSTING

½ cup butter, softened
2 cups powdered sugar
1 teaspoon vanilla
3 egg yolks
½ of 4 oz. bar (4 sections)
   GHIRARDELLI UNSWEETENED
   BAKING CHOCOLATE

Cream butter with sugar and vanilla. Add egg yolks one at a time, beating well after each addition. Beat until very fluffy. Melt chocolate according to package directions. Add to creamed mixture; beat on high speed until thick. Spread over top and sides of Telegraph Hill Chocolate Cake. Chill to firm frosting.

93

When the chips are down, this is the all-American cookie! . . .

GHIRARDELLI CHOCOLATE CHIP COOKIES

½ cup butter or margarine
½ cup sugar
¼ cup packed brown sugar
1 teaspoon vanilla
1 egg
1 cup plus 2 tablespoons unsifted
  flour
½ teaspoon salt
½ teaspoon baking soda
1 package (6 oz.) GHIRARDELLI
  SEMI-SWEET CHOCOLATE CHIPS
½ cup chopped walnuts

Cream butter with sugar, brown sugar and vanilla; beat in egg. Mix flour with salt and soda; mix into creamed mixture. Stir in Chocolate Chips and nuts. Drop by teaspoon onto greased baking sheet. Bake at 375°F for 8–10 minutes. Makes 4 dozen cookies.

FREEZE-EASY CHOCOLATE CHIP COOKIES

Prepare a double batch of Ghirardelli Chocolate Chip Cookies. Bake as many cookies as desired. Chill remaining dough for ½ hour. Shape dough into roll, 2 inches in diameter. Wrap in plastic wrap. Refrigerate for 1 week or freeze for longer. Frozen rolls should be thawed 30 minutes before slicing. When ready to bake, slice roll into 1 inch sections; cut each into 4 pieces. Bake as directed above.

Rich, chewy brownies with easy, two minute method . . .

GHIRARDELLI SQUARE FUDGE BROWNIES

½ cup butter or margarine, softened
¾ cup packed brown sugar
1 teaspoon vanilla
¼ teaspoon salt
2 eggs
¾ cup GHIRARDELLI GROUND
    CHOCOLATE
½ cup flour
½ cup chopped walnuts

Cream butter with brown sugar, vanilla and salt (just until blended); beat in eggs. Mix in Ground Chocolate. (Do not overmix.) Total mixing time is about 2 minutes. Scrape down bowl; stir in flour and nuts. Spread into greased 8 or 9-inch square pan. Bake at 350°F for 20–25 minutes. For extra chewy brownies, use 8-inch pan and less baking time. For cakelike brownies, use 9-inch pan and longer baking time. Cool on rack. Frost if desired. Cut into squares. Makes 20 servings.

FUDGE BROWNIE PIE

Prepare Ghirardelli Square Fudge Brownies without nuts. Spread into greased 9-inch round pie pan. Sprinkle top with the chopped nuts, ⅓ cup Ghirardelli Semi-Sweet Chocolate Chips and 1 teaspoon sugar. Bake 25–28 minutes. Cool and cut into wedges. Top each serving with scoop of ice cream. Drizzle with chocolate syrup too, if desired. Makes 8 servings.

A popular recipe for generations—this rich butter cookie surrounds chocolate mint wafer . . .

STARLIGHT MINT SURPRISE COOKIES

½ cup butter or margarine
½ cup granulated sugar
¼ cup packed brown sugar
1 egg
1 tablespoon water
½ teaspoon vanilla
1½ cups unsifted flour
½ teaspoon baking soda
¼ teaspoon salt
1 box (5 oz.) GHIRARDELLI MINT
  CHOCOLATE WAFERS
36 walnut halves

Cream butter with sugar and brown sugar. Mix in egg, water and vanilla. Stir flour with soda and salt; add to creamed mixture. Chill at least 2 hours. Enclose one Mint Chocolate Wafer in each rounded teaspoon of dough. Place on greased baking sheet; top each cookie with a walnut half. Bake at 375°F for 8–10 minutes. Cool on wire rack. Makes 3 dozen cookies.

A double pleasure for chocoholics . . .

FUDGY CHOCOLATE CHIP COOKIES

1 package (12 oz.) GHIRARDELLI
   SEMI-SWEET CHOCOLATE CHIPS
½ cup butter or margarine
1 egg
½ cup sugar
½ cup packed brown sugar
1 teaspoon vanilla
1⅔ cups flour
½ teaspoon baking soda
½ teaspoon baking powder
½ teaspoon salt
¼ cup milk
1 teaspoon lemon juice
½ cup chopped walnuts

In heavy saucepan, melt 1 cup Chocolate Chips with butter, stirring constantly. Beat egg with sugar, brown sugar and vanilla until creamed. Mix in melted chocolate. Stir flour with baking soda, baking powder and salt. Combine milk with lemon juice, stirring until thick. Add dry ingredients to chocolate mixture alternately with milk. Stir in nuts and remaining cup Chocolate Chips. Chill dough. Drop by teaspoon onto ungreased baking sheet. Bake at 350°F for 8–10 minutes. Cool on rack. Makes 4 dozen cookies.

A way to a man's heart is through a chocolate brownie . . .

BROWN VELVET FROSTED BROWNIES

⅓ cup butter or margarine, softened
1 cup sugar
2 eggs
½ teaspoon vanilla
½ teaspoon salt
4 sections (2 oz.) GHIRARDELLI UNSWEETENED BAKING CHOCOLATE
½ cup unsifted flour
½ cup chopped walnuts

By hand, lightly cream butter with sugar. Mix in eggs, vanilla and salt. Melt chocolate according to package directions. Stir melted chocolate into creamed mixture. Add flour, mixing until smooth; add nuts. Spread into greased 8 or 9-inch square pan. Bake at 350°F for 20–25 minutes. For extrafudgy brownies, use 8-inch pan or less baking time. For cakelike brownies, use 9-inch pan or longer baking time. Cool in pan. Frost with half recipe Dark Chocolate Frosting. Cut into squares. Makes 20–25 squares.

DARK CHOCOLATE FROSTING

4 sections (2 oz.) GHIRARDELLI UNSWEETENED BAKING CHOCOLATE
¼ cup butter
¼ cup milk
Pinch salt
2½ cups powdered sugar
½ teaspoon vanilla

In heavy saucepan on low heat, melt broken chocolate with butter, milk and salt. Stir constantly until thick and smooth. Remove from heat. Mix in sugar and vanilla. Beat until thick enough to spread. Frosts 9 by 13-inch cake.

An easy recipe for children to make . . .

TRIPLE TREAT GHIRARDELLI SQUARES

1½ cups graham cracker crumbs
¼ cup brown sugar
6 tablespoons butter or margarine,
  melted
Pinch nutmeg
1 package (12 oz.) GHIRARDELLI
  SEMI-SWEET CHOCOLATE CHIPS
1 cup flaked coconut
1 cup chopped pecans or walnuts
1 jar (7 oz.) marshmallow creme
2 tablespoons milk
1 teaspoon vanilla

Combine crumbs, sugar and butter. Press into 9 by 13-inch pan. Bake at 350°F for 10 minutes; remove from oven. Mix Chocolate Chips with coconut and nuts. Spread over first layer. Thin marshmallow creme with milk and vanilla. Drizzle over top. Bake additional 15 minutes. Cool before cutting into squares. Makes 32 squares.

Black pepper in a cookie! . . .

CHOCOLATE PEPPER SNAPS

1 cup GHIRARDELLI GROUND
   CHOCOLATE
1½ cups unsifted flour
¼ teaspoon salt
1½ teaspoon baking powder
¾ cup butter or margarine
1½ teaspoons vanilla
¾ teaspoons cinnamon
¼ teaspoon black pepper
⅛ teaspoon ground cloves
¾ cup sugar
1 egg

Sift Ground Chocolate with flour, salt and baking powder. Cream butter with vanilla and spices; add sugar and egg. Beat until light and fluffy. Slowly add sifted ingredients to creamed mixture. Chill dough 30 minutes. Shape into 1-inch balls and flatten with a fork or use a cookie press. Place a Ghirardelli Chocolate Chip in the center of each cookie before baking, if desired. Bake on ungreased cookie sheet at 350°F 10–12 minutes. Makes 4 dozen cookies.

Easy 1-pan recipe for chewy brownies . . .

SAN QUENTIN FUDGE BARS

1 package (6 oz.) GHIRARDELLI
   SEMI-SWEET CHOCOLATE CHIPS
¼ cup shortening
1 cup packed brown sugar
2 eggs
1 teaspoon vanilla
½ teaspoon salt
1 cup flour
½ teaspoon baking powder
½ cup chopped nuts

In heavy saucepan or microwave oven, melt chocolate with shortening. Remove from heat. With wire whip, blend in brown sugar. Beat eggs lightly with vanilla and salt; stir into chocolate mixture in pan. Mix flour with baking powder. Add, all at once, beating until smooth. Spread into greased 9-inch square pan. Sprinkle nuts over top. Bake at 350°F for 20 minutes. Cool before cutting into bars. Makes 32 cookies.

Add to your collection of chocolate chip cookie recipes . . .

CABLE CAR CHOCOLATE CHIP COOKIES

½ cup butter or margarine, softened
¾ cup sugar
1 teaspoon vanilla
1 egg
1 cup unsifted flour
½ teaspoon salt
½ teaspoon baking soda
1 package (6 oz.) GHIRARDELLI
  SEMI-SWEET CHOCOLATE CHIPS
½ cup chopped pecans
⅓ cup chopped maraschino cherries

Cream butter with sugar and vanilla. Beat in egg. Stir flour with salt and baking soda. Mix dry ingredients into creamed mixture. Stir in Chocolate Chips, nuts and cherries. Drop by teaspoon onto greased baking sheet. Bake at 350°F for 10 minutes. Cool on rack. Makes 4 dozen cookies.

105

Light as a cloud floating with bits of mint . . .

MARINA MINT MERINGUES

2 egg whites
Pinch salt
½ teaspoon vanilla
⅔ cup sugar
½ package (1 cup) FLICK-ETTE MINT
  CHOCOLATE FLAVORED CHIPS

Preheat oven to 375°F. Beat egg whites with salt and vanilla until foamy. Add sugar slowly, beating on high speed about 2 minutes or until sugar is dissolved and egg whites are very stiff. Fold in Flick-ettes. Drop by teaspoon onto greased baking sheet. Place meringues in oven and turn off heat. Leave in oven 1 hour or longer. Makes 32 cookies.

If you like the candy, you'll love these cookies! . . .

COOKIE TURTLES

½ cup butter or margarine
1 cup packed brown sugar
1 egg
½ teaspoon maple flavoring
1 cup unsifted flour
1 teaspoon baking powder
½ teaspoon salt
Pecan halves
1 package (6 oz.) GHIRARDELLI
  SEMI-SWEET CHOCOLATE CHIPS
2 tablespoons milk

Cream butter with sugar. Add egg and maple flavoring, beating until smooth. Stir flour with baking powder and salt; blend into creamed mixture. Chill dough. Drop dough by teaspoon onto ungreased baking sheet. Push 3 pecan halves into bottom edge of each cookie, forming a triangle with nuts. Bake at 350°F for 12–14 minutes. Cool on rack. In double boiler, melt Chocolate Chips with milk, stirring constantly, over 1-inch simmering water. Frost top of cookie with melted chocolate. Makes 3 dozen cookies.

Giant chocolate chip cookies are shaped with an ice cream scoop . . .

FLAP JACK COOKIES

½ cup butter or margarine, softened
½ cup packed dark brown sugar
⅓ cup sugar
1 egg
1 teaspoon vanilla
1 cup unsifted flour
½ teaspoon baking powder
½ teaspoon salt
¼ teaspoon cinnamon
¾ cup quick rolled oats
1 packed (6 oz.) GHIRARDELLI SEMI-
    SWEET CHOCOLATE CHIPS

Cream butter lightly with brown sugar and sugar. Mix in egg and vanilla. Stir flour with baking powder, salt and cinnamon. Add dry ingredients, rolled oats and Chocolate Chips. (Do not overmix.) Use ice-cream scoop to drop cookies onto greased baking sheets. Flatten with pancake turner dipped lightly in flour. Bake at 375°F for 10–12 minutes. Makes 12 (4-inch) cookies.

Nutritious cereal cookie for handy breakfast or snack . . . Freeze the leftovers . . .

SUTTER'S GOLD CHOCOLATE CHIP COOKIES

1 cup butter or margarine, softened
½ cup sugar
½ cup packed brown sugar
2 eggs
2 tablespoons milk
1 teaspoon vanilla
2 cups unsifted flour
1 teaspoon baking powder
½ teaspoon baking soda
½ teaspoon salt
1 package (12 oz.) GHIRARDELLI
  SEMI-SWEET CHOCOLATE CHIPS
3 cups breakfast wheat cereal flakes
Cinnamon sugar

Cream butter with sugar, brown sugar, eggs, milk and vanilla. Stir flour with baking powder, baking soda and salt; blend into creamed mixture. Stir in Chocolate Chips and cereal. Drop by teaspoon onto greased baking sheet. Sprinkle with cinnamon sugar. Bake at 350°F for 10 minutes. Cool on rack. Makes 6 dozen cookies.

BAKER BEACH PICNIC COOKIES

Follow recipe for Sutter's Gold Chocolate Chip Cookies, substituting 2 cups crushed potato chips for wheat cereal flakes. Bake as directed above.

Chocolate chip cookies have gone bananas . . .

GOLDEN NUGGET COOKIES

¾ **cup butter or margarine**
1 **cup sugar**
1 **egg**
½ **teaspoon vanilla**
½ **teaspoon cinnamon**
½ **teaspoon nutmeg**
1 **cup mashed ripe bananas**
1½ **cups flour**
½ **teaspoon salt**
½ **teaspoon baking soda**
1 **cup quick rolled oats**
1 **package (6 oz.) GHIRARDELLI
SEMI-SWEET CHOCOLATE CHIPS**

Cream butter with sugar, egg, vanilla, cinnamon and nutmeg. Mix in bananas. Combine flour, salt and baking soda; stir into creamed mixture. Fold in oats and Chocolate Chips. Drop by teaspoon onto greased baking sheet. Bake at 375°F for 8–10 minutes. Cool on rack. Makes 3 dozen cookies.

Mini fruit cakes delicious enough to serve any season of the year . . .

YULETIDE CHOCOLATE CHIP COOKIES

½ cup butter or margarine, softened
⅔ cup packed brown sugar
1 teaspoon brandy flavoring
3 tablespoons dark corn syrup
1 egg
1 cup diced candied mixed fruit
1⅓ cups flour
1 teaspoon pumpkin pie spice
¾ teaspoon baking powder
¼ teaspoon salt
1 package (6 oz.) GHIRARDELLI
    SEMI-SWEET CHOCOLATE CHIPS
⅓ cup chopped pecans
⅓ cup slivered almonds
⅓ cup currants
14 red candied cherries, quartered

Cream butter with brown sugar, brandy flavoring and corn syrup; add egg and beat until very light. Coat candied fruit with 1 tablespoon of the flour; set aside. Sift remaining flour with pumpkin pie spice, baking powder and salt. Stir dry ingredients into creamed mixture. Add fruit, Chocolate Chips, pecans, almonds and currants. Chill dough 1 hour. Drop by heaping teaspoon onto greased baking sheet. Top each cookie with piece of cherry. Bake at 350°F for 8–10 minutes. Cool on rack. Store in covered container several days to soften and age. Makes 4½ dozen cookies.

Crisscross marks the spot for the hidden milk chocolate wafer . . .

LONE MT. CHOCOLATE PEANUT TREASURES

½ cup butter or margarine, softened
½ cup chunky peanut butter
½ cup packed dark brown sugar
½ cup sugar
1 egg
1½ cups unsifted flour
½ teaspoon baking soda
1 box (5 oz.) GHIRARDELLI MILK
    CHOCOLATE WAFERS

Cream butter with peanut butter, brown sugar and sugar; beat in egg. (Do not overmix.) Combine flour with baking soda; stir into creamed mixture. Chill dough 1 hour. Shape cookies by enclosing one Milk Chocolate Wafer in each rounded teaspoon of dough. Place on greased baking sheet. Crisscross top with fork. Bake at 350°F for 8–10 minutes. Cool on wire rack. Makes 4 dozen cookies.

A fast recipe for the working woman . . .

ALHAMBRA CHOCOLATE DOT MACAROONS

3 egg whites
¼ teaspoon salt
¼ teaspoon cream of tartar
1 cup sugar
1 teaspoon vanilla
2 cups flaked coconut
1 package (6 oz.) GHIRARDELLI
    SEMI-SWEET CHOCOLATE CHIPS

Beat egg whites until foamy. Add salt and cream of tartar; continue beating until soft peaks form. Gradually add sugar and vanilla, beating until stiff. Fold in coconut and Chocolate Chips. Drop by teaspoon onto foil-covered baking sheet. Bake at 300°F for 20 minutes. Cool completely. Pull cookies from foil. Makes 4 dozen cookies.

Jump on the bandwagon with crisp peanut cookies . . .

PEANUT BUTTER CHOCOLATE CHIP COOKIES

½ cup peanut butter
½ cup butter or margarine, softened
½ cup packed brown sugar
¼ cup sugar
1 teaspoon vanilla
1 egg
1 tablespoon water
1 cup unsifted flour
½ teaspoon salt
½ teaspoon baking powder
¾ cup chopped peanuts
1 package (6 oz.) GHIRARDELLI
   SEMI-SWEET CHOCOLATE CHIPS

Cream peanut butter with butter, adding brown sugar, sugar, vanilla, egg and water. Stir flour with salt and baking powder. Gradually add dry ingredients to creamed mixture. Stir in peanuts and Chocolate Chips. Drop by teaspoon onto ungreased baking sheet. To flatten cookies, crisscross with fork. Bake at 350°F for 10–12 minutes. Cool on rack. Makes 5 dozen cookies.

Chocolate and peanut butter team up for the Giants ball game . . .

FRISCO CHOCOLATE PEANUT BUTTER COOKIES

½ cup butter or margarine, softened
½ cup peanut butter
⅓ cup packed brown sugar
1 egg
½ cup sugar
½ cup GHIRARDELLI GROUND
   CHOCOLATE
1⅓ cups unsifted flour
½ teaspoon baking soda
½ teaspoon teaspoon salt

Cream butter with peanut butter. Mix in brown sugar and egg. Blend sugar with Ground Chocolate; add to creamed mixture. Stir flour with baking soda and salt. Gradually add dry ingredients, mixing thoroughly. Chill 20 minutes to firm dough. Roll into 1-inch balls. Place on greased baking sheet and flatten with fork or fancy potato masher. Bake at 350°F for 10–12 minutes. Cool on wire rack. Makes 4 dozen cookies.

Slice the pinwheel for a touch of mint . . .

CHOCOLATE MINT WINDMILL COOKIES

1 bar (4 oz.) GHIRARDELLI
   SEMI-SWEET CHOCOLATE
½ cup butter or margarine, softened
½ cup sugar
¼ cup packed brown sugar
1 egg
¼ cup sour cream
2 cups unsifted flour
½ teaspoon baking powder
½ teaspoon salt
⅛ baking soda
1 teaspoon vanilla
¼ teaspoon peppermint extract
3 drops green or red food coloring

In double boiler, melt chocolate over 1-inch simmering water. Cream butter with sugar and brown sugar; mix in egg and sour cream. Stir flour with baking powder, salt and baking soda. Gradually add dry ingredients to creamed mixture. Divide dough in half. Add melted chocolate and vanilla to half. Add peppermint extract and food coloring to other half. Chill dough. Between 2 pieces of waxed paper, roll each half into a rectangle ⅛ inch thick. Place peppermint half on top of chocolate half and roll as for jelly roll. Wrap in waxed paper; chill. Cut in ¼-inch slices. Place on ungreased baking sheet. Bake at 375°F for 8–10 minutes. Makes 3½ dozen cookies.

On the trail or in the camp, be sure to pack this tasty snack ...

REDWOOD CAMP COOKIES

½ cup butter or margarine
¼ cup sugar
½ cup packed brown sugar
2 eggs, beaten
1½ teaspoons vanilla
½ cup quick rolled oats
1 cup unsifted flour
½ teaspoon baking soda
¼ teaspoon salt
⅛ teaspoon cinnamon
½ cup chopped peanuts
1 package (6 oz.) GHIRARDELLI
   SEMI-SWEET CHOCOLATE CHIPS

Lightly cream butter with sugar and brown sugar. Add eggs and vanilla. (Mixture will be lumpy.) Stir flour with baking soda, salt and cinnamon. Mix dry ingredients into creamed mixture. Fold in peanuts and Chocolate Chips. Spread dough into greased 9 by 13-inch baking pan. Bake at 350°F for about 20 minutes. Cool before cutting into squares. To keep moist, wrap in foil. Makes 24 (2-inch) squares.

The natural flavor comes through with homemade granola . . .

HAIGHT-ASHBURY GRANOLA COOKIES

1 cup regular rolled oats
2 tablespoons oil
½ cup butter or margarine, softened
½ cup honey
½ cup packed brown sugar
1 egg
¼ cup wheat germ
1 teaspoon vanilla
1½ teaspoons cinnamon
¼ teaspoon allspice
1½ cups unbleached flour
¾ teaspoon salt
½ teaspoon baking powder
½ teaspoon baking soda
¼ cup milk
¾ cup chopped dates
¾ cup chopped walnuts
¾ cup flaked coconut
1 package (6 oz.) GHIRARDELLI
  SEMI-SWEET CHOCOLATE CHIPS

In baking pan, toss oats with oil. Toast oats at 350°F for 15 minutes, stirring once. Cream butter with honey, brown sugar, egg, vanilla and spices. Mix in wheat germ. Stir flour with salt, baking powder and baking soda. Mix dry ingredients into creamed mixture alternately with milk. Stir in toasted oats, dates, nuts, coconut and Chocolate Chips. Drop by teaspoon onto greased baking sheet. Bake at 350°F for 9–10 minutes. Cool on rack. Makes 7 dozen cookies.

A fun recipe for the whole family . . .

NUTTY CHOCOLATE DIPPED PRETZELS OR MARSHMALLOWS

1 package (12 oz.) GHIRARDELLI
SEMI-SWEET CHOCOLATE CHIPS
3 tablespoons shortening
Twisted pretzels or large
marshmallows
1 cup finely chopped walnuts
(optional)

In double boiler, melt chocolate with shortening over 1-inch simmering water, stirring constantly, or microwave 2–3 minutes on medium; stir until smooth. Do not overheat. Chocolate should be lukewarm. Drop pretzels or marshmallows into chocolate mixture one at a time. (3-inch pretzels work best, but large pretzels may also be used.) Remove with a fork, draining excess chocolate. Dip pretzel or marshmallow into nuts spread flat on a plate. Lay on waxed paper-lined flat pan. Chill until very firm at least 1 hour. When ready to serve, remove from paper.

NOTE: Chocolate will melt if room temperature is above 72–75°F.

A unique taste of the Orient in San Francisco . . .

CHINATOWN SESAME COOKIES

½ cup butter or margarine
¼ cup sugar
1 egg
2 tablespoons molasses
⅓ cup lukewarm milk
½ cup GHIRARDELLI GROUND
    CHOCOLATE
2 cups unsifted flour
1 teaspoon baking powder
½ teaspoon salt
¼ teaspoon ginger
¾ cup sesame seeds

Cream butter with sugar, egg and molasses. Stir milk with Ground Chocolate; add to creamed mixture. Stir flour with baking powder, salt and ginger. Gradually add dry ingredients to creamed mixture, stirring until blended. Chill dough 1 hour. Shape into small balls the size of walnuts. Roll in sesame seeds. Place on greased baking sheets. Flatten with spatula. Bake at 375°F for 10 minutes. Makes 3 dozen cookies.

My favorite cookie for everyone . . .

CHERRY CORDIAL COOKIES

1 package (12 oz.) GHIRARDELLI
   SEMI-SWEET CHOCOLATE CHIPS
½ cup butter or margarine
1 cup packed brown sugar
1 egg
1 teaspoon vanilla
2 cups unsifted flour
1 teaspoon baking powder
½ teaspoon salt
1 jar (16 oz.) maraschino cherries
2 tablespoons maraschino cherry
   syrup
1 tablespoon butter or margarine

In double boiler, melt 1 cup Chocolate Chips over 1-inch simmering water. Cream ½ cup butter with sugar. Add egg, vanilla and melted chocolate; beat until smooth. Combine flour with baking powder and salt; add to creamed mixture, beating until smooth. Chill at least 1 hour. Enclose 1 cherry in 1 tablespoon dough. Place on greased baking sheet. Bake at 350°F for 12–14 minutes. Cool on wire rack.

Frosting
Melt remaining cup Chocolate Chips with maraschino cherry syrup and 1 tablespoon butter. Frost top of cookies. Makes approximately 3½ dozen cookies.

Famous from Ghirardelli Square . . .

GHIRARDELLI HOT FUDGE SAUCE

1 package (10 oz.) GHIRARDELLI
  MILK CHOCOLATE BLOCKS
⅓ to ½ cup milk
1 teaspoon vanilla

In heavy saucepan, break Chocolate Blocks into hot milk. (For thick sauce, use ⅓ cup milk.) Stir constantly until sauce is smooth; add vanilla. To microwave: In glass measuring cup, melt broken chocolate with milk for 2–3 minutes on MEDIUM, stirring twice until very smooth; add vanilla. Serve warm over ice cream. Makes 1¼ cups sauce.

SAUSALITO CHOCOLATE MUD PIE

Crust
25 chocolate sandwich cookies
½ cup finely chopped walnuts
2 tablespoons butter

Filling
½ gallon coffee ice cream
¼ cup crème de cacao
GHIRARDELLI HOT FUDGE SAUCE
  (Recipe above)

Crust
Crush cookies to make 2 cups crumbs. Mix in nuts. Cut in butter. (Food processor is best for making crust.) With back of large spoon, press crumbs into 9-inch square pan or pie pan.

Filling
Place slightly soft ice cream in large bowl. Stir liqueur into ice cream, mixing lightly. Fill crust with ice cream. Smooth top with metal spatula. Freeze until firm. Prepare Hot Fudge Sauce using ½ cup milk. Cool sauce and then pour over ice cream. Cover and freeze until ready to serve. Thaw slightly before cutting. Makes 8–9 servings.

A chocolate Sundae for every day of the week . . .

GOLD STREET CHOCOLATE SAUCE

½ of 4 oz. bar (4 sections)
  GHIRARDELLI SEMI-SWEET
  CHOCOLATE
¼ cup orange marmalade
¼ cup honey
3 tablespoons Triple Sec or orange
  liqueur

In heavy saucepan or microwave oven, melt broken chocolate with orange marmalade, honey and orange liqueur. Stir until smooth. Serve over Aunt Lottie's Pound Cake (page 91), ice cream or custard.

MOCHA VELVET SAUCE

½ of 4 oz. bar (4 sections)
  GHIRARDELLI SEMI-SWEET
  CHOCOLATE
½ cup light corn syrup
½ teaspoon instant coffee
¼ cup Kahlua or coffee liqueur

In heavy saucepan or microwave oven, melt broken chocolate with corn syrup, coffee and liqueur. Stir until smooth. Serve over ice cream or chocolate cake.

From A to Z with Chocolate . . .

CHOCOLATE ZABAGLIONE SAUCE

½ of 4 oz. bar (4 sections)
   GHIRARDELLI SEMI-SWEET
   CHOCOLATE
½ cup Marsala wine
⅓ cup sugar
2 egg yolks, well beaten

In heavy saucepan, combine broken chocolate, wine and sugar; heat, stirring until blended. Heat to boiling; cook one minute. Remove from heat. With wire whip, quickly stir in egg yolks. Return saucepan to low heat; stir until slightly thickened. Serve sauce warm or cold over Mt. Shasta Baked Alaska (page 85), strawberries or other fresh fruit.

CHOCOLATE WHIPPED CREAM TOPPING

124

½ pint whipping cream
¼ cup GHIRARDELLI INSTANT
   CHOCOLATE FLAVOR DRINK
½ teaspoon vanilla

Combine whipping cream, vanilla and Instant Chocolate Flavor Drink. Whip until thick. Serve as topping for cakes, puddings or pies.

More delicious toppings . . .

CHOCOLAT DE MENTHE SAUCE

½ of 4 oz. bar (4 sections)
  GHIRARDELLI SEMI-SWEET
  CHOCOLATE
½ cup light corn syrup
¼ cup white crème de menthe

In heavy saucepan or microwave oven, melt broken chocolate with corn syrup and crème de menthe. Stir until smooth. Serve with ice cream or over Chocolaty Cream Puffs (page 133). Makes one cup sauce.

MORTON STREET RUMMY SAUCE

½ of 4 oz. bar (4 sections)
  GHIRARDELLI SEMI-SWEET
  CHOCOLATE
¼ cup honey
¼ cup light corn syrup
3 tablespoons rum
1 tablespoon brandy

In heavy saucepan or microwave oven, melt broken chocolate with honey, corn syrup, rum and brandy. Stir until smooth. Serve over steam pudding or St. Francis Dark Fruit Cake (page 89).

125

Dip cubes of fresh fruit into melted chocolate. Spreads a little love with friends . . .

CHOCOLATE FONDUE DESSERT

6 squares (6 oz.) GHIRARDELLI MILK CHOCOLATE BLOCKS
1 bar (4 oz.) GHIRARDELLI SEMI-SWEET CHOCOLATE
½ cup vanilla ice cream
3 tablespoons liqueur (any flavor) or sweet wine
Chilled fresh fruit: Strawberries, bananas, pineapple, pears, grapes, oranges.

Fondue may be prepared in a fondue pot, heavy saucepan or double boiler. Break chocolate into small pieces. Melt chocolate with ice cream and liqueur, stirring constantly for a smooth sauce. Or microwave all ingredients on MEDIUM 3–4 minutes, stirring 3 times. Cool sauce slightly before serving. If sauce is too hot, chocolate will run off fruit. Makes about 1 cup sauce.

This dessert may be prepared in advance and kept warm in a double boiler. At dessert time, serve a bowl of chocolate fondue surrounded by chilled fresh fruit. Guests use forks to dip fruit. Children may like to dip pretzels or large marshmallows. Leftover fondue may be used for a sauce over ice cream; thin with milk or cream to desired consistency.

NOTE: Any type Ghirardelli Milk Chocolate and Semi-Sweet Chocolate may be substituted in this recipe.

A dark chocolate mousse with sour cream . . .

BLACK FOREST CHOCOLATE MOUSSE

**2 bars (4 oz. each) GHIRARDELLI
SEMI-SWEET CHOCOLATE**
2 tablespoons warm water
1 cup whipping cream
¾ cup sugar
Pinch salt
3 tablespoons Kirsch (cherry liqueur)
½ cup sour cream
6 whole maraschino cherries

In double boiler, melt chocolate with water over 1-inch simmering water, stirring until smooth. Whip cream with sugar and salt. Gradually add melted chocolate and Kirsch, beating at low speed until smooth. Fold in sour cream. Spoon into serving dishes. Drop one cherry on side of each dessert dish. Chill. Makes 6 (½ cup) servings.

127

The "In" dessert is now chocolate mousse . . .

Union Square Chocolate Mousse

4 sections (2 oz.) GHIRARDELLI
   UNSWEETENED BAKING
   CHOCOLATE
¼ cup hot water
⅔ cup sugar
2 eggs, separated (room temperature)
Pinch salt
½ cup whipping cream

In heavy saucepan on low heat, melt broken chocolate with water and ⅓ cup sugar, stirring until thick and smooth (about 10 minutes). Beat egg yolks until very thick and light colored. Quickly stir egg yolks into chocolate mixture; remove from heat. Beat egg whites with salt until foamy. Gradually add remaining ⅓ cup sugar, beating until soft peaks form. Fold chocolate mixture into egg whites. Whip cream until soft peaks form; fold into chocolate mixture. Pour into small stemmed glasses. Chill several hours or overnight. Decorate with additional whipped cream, if desired. Makes 6 (½ cup) servings.

Berry beautiful buffet dessert . . .

GOURMET CHOCOLATE DIPPED STRAWBERRIES

**1 basket large strawberries with
stems
2 bars (4 oz. each) GHIRARDELLI
SEMI-SWEET CHOCOLATE** .

Carefully rinse strawberries. Using paper towels, dry berries thoroughly. Break chocolate into sections. Finely chop 5 of the sections and reserve. Break remaining sections into double boiler over 1-inch simmering water. Stir constantly until melted and smooth. (Do not overheat.) Remove pan of chocolate. Add reserved finely chopped chocolate, stirring until smooth. Melted chocolate should be thick enough to hold a shape when stirred. Hold each strawberry by stem or a fork. Tilt the pan and use a spoon to coat each berry with chocolate. Hold each berry upside down to catch drips. Place in fluted foil cupcake liners or on pan covered with plastic wrap. Chill until firm or freeze a few minutes to serve immediately. Makes about 12 servings.

129

Chocolate version of the ever popular crepe . . .

CHOCOLATE CREPES

½ of 4 oz. bar (4 sections)
  **GHIRARDELLI SEMI-SWEET
  CHOCOLATE**
1 tablespoons butter or margarine
1 cup milk
2 eggs
2 tablespoons sugar
1 tablespoon brandy
¼ teaspoon salt
1 cup unsifted flour

In heavy saucepan, melt broken chocolate with butter, stirring constantly. In blender, combine milk, eggs, sugar, brandy and salt; blend in flour. Add chocolate mixture, blending until smooth. Chill at least 2 hours. Season 6-inch crepe pan with oil; wipe out excess and melt a small amount of butter. Remove pan from heat and pour a heaping tablespoon batter quickly into crepe pan. Roll pan to spread batter over bottom of pan. Cook on medium high heat; turn to brown both sides. Make crepes as thin as possible. Add additional butter for every other crepe. If batter should become too thick, add cold water as needed. Stack on plate, covering with damp paper towel. Crepes may be made in advance. Wrap in plastic and store in refrigerator or freezer. To reheat, wrap in foil and heat at 350°F for 5 minutes. Makes 16 crepes.

French dessert from San Francisco . . .

CREPES ANNETTE

3 tablespoons sugar
1 teaspoon grated orange peel
¼ teaspoon grated lemon peel
3 tablespoons butter
½ cup orange juice
¼ cup orange liqueur
¼ cup brandy
½ of 4 oz. bar (4 sections)
  GHIRARDELLI SEMI-SWEET
  CHOCOLATE
16 Chocolate Crepes
  (page 130)

In chafing dish or large skillet, heat sugar with orange and lemon peel. Stir constantly for a few minutes. (Do not melt sugar.) Stir in butter and melt. Add orange juice, liqueur and brandy. Cook until slightly thickened. Fold Chocolate Crepes into fourths. Heat crepes in sauce. Serve 2 crepes with sauce for each serving. Decorate top with grated chocolate, if desired.

CREPES PACIFICA

½ of 4 oz. bar (4 sections)
  GHIRARDELLI SEMI-SWEET
  CHOCOLATE
½ cup hot water
¼ cup packed brown sugar
Dash salt
½ teaspoon vanilla extract or brandy
  flavoring
16 Chocolate Crepes (page 130)
1 quart chocolate chip ice cream

Chocolate Sauce
In heavy saucepan, combine broken chocolate, water, sugar and salt. Heat to boiling; reduce heat and simmer 2–3 minutes. Cool sauce and add vanilla.

Fill each crepe with ¼ cup ice cream; fold over. Serve 2 crepes topped with the chocolate sauce.

An easy chafing dish dessert to impress your guests . . .

BANANAS CORTEZ

2 bananas
¼ cup butter
3 tablespoons GHIRARDELLI
  GROUND CHOCOLATE
¼ cup packed brown sugar
3 tablespoons Amaretto or banana
  liqueur
1 pint vanilla ice cream

Cut each banana lengthwise and then in half, making 8 pieces. In 10-inch skillet or chafing dish, sauté bananas in 2 tablespoons melted butter until golden brown. Add remaining butter. Mix Ground Chocolate with sugar and liqueur. Push bananas to side of pan. Stir chocolate mixture into melted butter. Simmer until sauce is smooth and bubbly. Divide ice cream onto 4 plates. Spoon bananas and sauce over top. Makes 4 servings.

Personalize these puffs with your favorite filling . . .

CHOCOLATY CREAM PUFFS

1 cup boiling water
½ cup butter
1 cup unsifted flour
¼ cup GHIRARDELLI GROUND
   CHOCOLATE
¼ teaspoon salt
4 eggs

In saucepan, combine water, butter, Ground Chocolate and salt; heat to boiling. Add flour, all at once, to liquid. Cook, stirring constantly until mixture forms a ball that does not separate. Remove from heat; cool 10 minutes. Add eggs, 1 at a time, beating vigorously for 1 minute after each addition. Drop dough by heaping tablespoon or ice cream scoop on heavily greased baking sheet. Bake at 400°F for 20 minutes. Cool on rack. Split puffs with sharp knife. Fill with ice cream, whipped cream or pudding. Top with Chocolate de Menthe Sauce (page 125), if desired. Makes 16 puffs.

Be your own French chef with this perfect soufflé . . .

GRAND MARNIER SOUFFLÉ WITH CHOCOLATE SAUCE

3 tablespoons butter
4½ tablespoons flour
1½ cups milk
6 eggs, separated
½ cup sugar
3 tablespoons Grand Marnier
Pinch salt
⅛ teaspoon cream of tartar

Butter sides of 1½-quart soufflé dish; sprinkle with sugar. Arrange foil collar with tape around outside; butter collar. Preheat oven to 400°F. In saucepan, melt butter; blend in flour. Add milk and sugar; heat to boiling. Remove from heat. Add egg yolks, 1 at a time, beating with wire whip. Stir in Grand Marnier. Whip egg whites with salt and cream of tartar until stiff. Fold ⅓ egg whites into sauce; fold sauce into remaining egg whites, moving bowl quarter turn each fold. Pour mixture into soufflé dish. Reduce oven heat to 375°F. Bake about 30 minutes. Serve immediately with Marnier Chocolate Sauce.

134

MARNIER CHOCOLATE SAUCE

½ of 4 oz. bar (4 sections)
  GHIRARDELLI SEMI-SWEET
  CHOCOLATE
½ cup half and half
1 tablespoon sugar
1 egg yolk, beaten
2 tablespoons Grand Marnier

In double boiler, melt broken chocolate with half and half and sugar. Using wire whip, quickly stir in egg yolk. Add Grand Marnier. Cook until sauce is thick. Serve hot or cold over Grand Marnier Soufflé.

Pears smothered in chocolate baked with crunchy topping . . .

CHOCOLATE POIRE

1 can (29 oz.) pear halves
2 tablespoons brown sugar
½ teaspoon cinnamon
1 teaspoon vanilla
1 package (6 oz.) GHIRARDELLI
   SEMI-SWEET CHOCOLATE CHIPS
¾ cup flour
¼ cup sugar
½ teaspoon baking powder
¼ teaspoon salt
¼ cup butter or margarine
⅓ cup chopped pecans
¼ cup quick rolled oats

Drain pears, reserving syrup. Place pears in heavily buttered 9-inch square pan. Combine pear syrup with brown sugar, cinnamon and vanilla; pour over pears. Sprinkle Chocolate Chips over pears in syrup. Combine flour, sugar, baking powder and salt. With pastry blender, cut in butter until mixture is very fine. Add nuts and oats. Sprinkle topping over pears. Bake at 375°F for 35 minutes. Cool slightly and cut into squares. Garnish with whipped cream, if desired. Makes 6 servings.

Holiday steamed pudding with almonds and figs . . .

TRADITIONAL CHOCOLATE FIG PUDDING

⅓ cup butter or margarine, softened
½ cup sugar
2 eggs
1 teaspoon vanilla
¾ cup GHIRARDELLI GROUND
  CHOCOLATE
½ cup ground almonds
1⅓ cups unsifted flour
½ teaspoon salt
¼ teaspoon baking soda
¼ teaspoon cream of tartar
1 cup milk
½ cup diced dried black figs

In small mixer bowl, cream butter with sugar; beat in eggs and vanilla. Add Ground Chocolate and almonds, whipping until fluffy. Sift flour with salt, soda and cream of tartar. Add dry ingredients alternately with milk, mixing until smooth. Fold in figs. Pour into buttered 1½-quart mold or metal bowl. Place pudding mold on rack in pan of 1-inch boiling water. Cover water pan tightly and steam on low heat for 1 hour. Unmold. Serve warm with whipped cream, if desired. Pudding may be made days in advance. Reheat in steamer as directed above. Serves 8.

Brownie custard pleases everyone ...

RICHMOND CHOCOLATE BREAD PUDDING

½ cup GHIRARDELLI GROUND
   CHOCOLATE
⅓ cup sugar
¼ teaspoon salt
Pinch cinnamon
2 cups milk, scalded
2 eggs, slightly beaten
1½ teaspoons vanilla
2 slices dry French bread
¼ cup raisins

Blend Ground Chocolate with sugar, salt and cinnamon. Dissolve chocolate mixture in hot milk. Stir in eggs, vanilla, crumbled bread and raisins. Pour into 8-inch square pan. Set in a larger pan of warm water. Bake at 350°F for 30 minutes or until set. Cool and cut into squares. Garnish with whipped cream and nutmeg, if desired. Makes 6 servings.

137

SHERRIED CHOCOLATE CUSTARD

1¾ cups milk
1 bar (4 oz.) GHIRARDELLI
   SEMI-SWEET CHOCOLATE
2 eggs, slightly beaten
¼ cup sugar
1 tablespoon sweet sherry wine
Pinch salt

Scald milk; remove from heat. Break chocolate into hot milk; stir until melted. Blend in eggs, sugar, sherry and salt. Pour into 6 custard cups. Place cups in pan with 1-inch hot water. Bake at 325°F for 40–45 minutes. Chill. Makes 6 servings.

Homemade goodness cranked into this frozen chocolate cream . . .

HOMEMADE CHOCOLATE ICE CREAM

2 bars (4 oz. each) GHIRARDELLI
   SEMI-SWEET CHOCOLATE
1 quart half and half
1½ cups sugar
¼ cup flour
½ teaspoon salt
6 eggs, beaten
3 cups whipping cream
1 tablespoon vanilla

In heavy saucepan, melt broken chocolate with half and half. Combine sugar, flour and salt; add to chocolate mixture and heat to boiling. With wire whip, quickly mix in eggs. Cook until thickened. Add whipping cream and vanilla; cool. Pour into ice cream canister which will be approximately ¾ full. Freeze in ice cream maker according to manufacturer's directions. When ice cream is frozen, remove dasher. Replace lid and repack with ice and salt. Cover freezer with newspaper or heavy material. Let stand ½–1 hour. Makes 3½ quarts ice cream.

ROCKY ROAD ICE CREAM

Prepare Homemade Chocolate Ice Cream; stir 3 cups miniature marshmallows and 1½ cups chopped walnuts into ice cream before freezing. When ice cream is frozen, remove dasher and stir to distribute marshmallows and nuts. Pack as directed above.

Double your flavor, double your fun with . . .

DOUBLE DUTCH CHOCOLATE PUDDING CAKE

Cake

¾ cup unsifted flour
¼ cup GHIRARDELLI GROUND CHOCOLATE
¼ cup sugar
2 teaspoons baking powder
¼ teaspoon salt
¼ cup chopped nuts
½ cup milk
1 teaspoon vanilla
4 tablespoons melted butter

Cake

Into buttered 2-quart baking dish, sift flour, Ground Chocolate, sugar, baking powder and salt. Add nuts. Mix milk with vanilla and butter; stir into dry ingredients.

Pudding

¼ cup GHIRARDELLI GROUND CHOCOLATE
¼ cup sugar
¼ cup packed brown sugar
¼ teaspoon salt
1½ cups boiling water

Pudding

Mix Ground Chocolate, sugar, brown sugar and salt with boiling water. Pour over cake batter. Do not stir again. Bake at 350°F for 35–40 minutes. Serve warm or cold with whipped cream, if desired. Makes 6 servings.

A classic Italian delicacy . . .

CANNOLI DI CIOCCOLATA

Shells
1½ cups flour
2 tablespoons GHIRARDELLI
   GROUND CHOCOLATE
¼ teaspoon salt
½ teaspoon baking powder
2 tablespoons butter
½ cup sweet sherry wine

Filling
8 ounces ricotta cheese
½ cup whipping cream
¼ cup powdered sugar
1 teaspoon vanilla
½ of 4 oz. bar (4 sections)
   GHIRARDELLI SEMI-SWEET
   CHOCOLATE
1 tablespoon finely chopped citron

Shells
Sift flour with Ground Chocolate, salt and baking powder. Cut in butter, gradually adding wine. Knead well. On floured board, roll dough to ¹⁄₁₆ inch thick.. Cut into 4-inch squares. With rolling pin, roll squares into ovals. Wrap each oval around aluminum cannoli tube. Seal edge with egg white. Fry two at a time in 350°F oil for 1–2 minutes. Hold tubes with chop sticks to drain. Cool 5 minutes on absorbent paper. Carefully remove from tubes. Shells may be made 5 days in advance and stored in tightly covered can. Makes 12 Cannoli Shells.

Filling
In blender, combine cheese, cream, sugar and vanilla. Grate chocolate. Fold grated chocolate and chopped citron into creamed mixture. Use pastry tube to fill Cannoli Shells. Dust with powdered sugar. Garnish with chocolate syrup. Fills 12 Cannoli Shells.

London's Big Ben Tower influenced this British favorite . . .

CLOCK TOWER CHOCOLATE TRIFLE

Party Chocolate sponge cake
  (page 87)
⅔ cup cream sherry
1 package (3¾ oz.) vanilla instant
  pudding mix
1 egg
1½ cups cold milk
½ cup half and half
1 package (12 oz.) frozen raspberries,
  thawed
2 bananas, sliced
½ pint whipping cream
3 tablespoons powdered sugar
1 teaspoon vanilla
¼ cup toasted slivered almonds

Prepare Party Chocolate Sponge Cake. Use half of the cake for this recipe. Cut cake into ¾ inch slices. In a decorative 9-inch glass bowl, arrange 3 slices cake on bottom and 8 slices standing around edge. Sprinkle with ¼ cup sherry. To prepare pudding, beat egg slightly; add milk, half and half and 2 tablespoons sherry. Add pudding mix, beating for 2 minutes; let stand 5 minutes to thicken. Spoon half of pudding over cake. Spread raspberries with syrup and one banana over pudding. Cover with cake slices sprinkled with remaining sherry. Top with pudding. End with layer of banana slices. Whip cream with sugar and vanilla until stiff. Spread over top and sprinkle with nuts. Chill 1 hour or overnight. Makes 8 servings.

A flaming dessert for a special holiday dinner . . .

MINCEMEAT CHOCOLATE SUNDAE

1 jar (28 oz.) prepared mincemeat
½ cup chopped walnuts
⅓ cup brandy
2 tablespoons GHIRARDELLI
   GROUND CHOCOLATE
1 quart ice cream

In saucepan or chafing dish, combine all ingredients except ice cream. Heat through. Flame with additional brandy, if desired. Serve over vanilla or eggnog ice cream. Makes 6 servings.

REAL MINCEMEAT PIE

Combine sauce ingredients for Mincemeat Chocolate Sundae with 1 cup cooked, minced roast beef. Spread filling into 9-inch unbaked pie shell. Cover with top crust and crimp edge. Cut design in top crust for air vents. Sprinkle lightly with sugar. Bake at 400°F for 35 minutes. Serve warm. Makes 6 servings.

Traditional Marsala Italian custard à la Chocolate . . .

BITTER-SWEET CHOCOLATE ZABAGLIONE

1 bar (4 oz.) GHIRARDELLI
  SEMI-SWEET CHOCOLATE
¼ cup half and half
5 egg yolks
⅓ cup sugar
½ cup Marsala wine

In heavy saucepan or microwave, melt broken chocolate with half and half; set aside to cool. In double boiler, over simmering water, beat egg yolks with hand mixer. Gradually add sugar, beating on high until creamy. Add Marsala, stirring to heat slightly. Beat on high until mixture starts to thicken. Remove from heat and continue beating until very thick. Stir ½ cup of egg yolk mixture into chocolate; fold the two mixtures together. Serve immediately. Makes 5 (½ cup) servings.

NOTE: Traditionally, this dessert is served soft and slightly warm in small stemmed glasses, but it may be served chilled. Decorate with whipped cream, if desired.

143

Beautiful soufflé with a kiss of Amaretto! . . .

COIT TOWER BAKED CHOCOLATE SOUFFLÉ

144

3 tablespoons butter
3 tablespoons flour
1 cup milk
½ cup sugar
1 bar (4 oz.) GHIRARDELLI SEMI-SWEET CHOCOLATE
5 egg yolks
2 tablespoons Amaretto liqueur
6 egg whites (room temperature)
¼ teaspoon salt
Pinch cream of tartar

Heavily butter 3-quart soufflé dish and sprinkle with 1 teaspoon sugar. Arrange buttered double collar around outside of dish, folding ends together. For best results, chill empty dish for ½ hour. Preheat oven to 425°F. Before starting, read full recipe carefully.

In heavy saucepan, melt butter; blend in flour and stir until bubbly. Add milk, ¼ cup of the sugar and broken chocolate. Cook on medium heat, stirring frequently, until smooth and thickened and mixture just starts to come to a boil. Beat the egg yolks with electric mixer until very thick and lemon colored. With wire whip, stir chocolate mixture quickly while adding egg yolks slowly. Pour into large bowl. Stir in liqueur.

For best soufflé results, beat egg whites with large wire whip in copper bowl; electric mixer may be used. Beat whites until foamy; mix in salt and cream of tartar, beating until soft peaks form. Gradually add remaining ¼ cup sugar, beating until stiff but not dry. Blend ¼ of egg whites into chocolate mixture. Pile remaining egg whites over chocolate mixture. Carefully fold mixtures together, cutting down center and turning bowl. (Do not overmix.)

Pour into prepared soufflé dish. Bake on lower rack of oven at 425°F for 10 minutes. Lower heat to 350°F and bake for 25–30 minutes or until toothpick comes out clean. A few cracks will form on top. After a few minutes, remove collar. Serve immediately. Serve plain or with amaretto Creme Sauce. Makes 6 servings.

AMARETTO CREME SAUCE

Soften 1 cup vanilla ice cream with 3 tablespoons Amaretto liqueur. Serve in pitcher to pour over Coit Tower Baked Chocolate Soufflé.

Easy blender method for Italian chocolate cream dessert . . .

CIOCCOLATINO ALLA CREMA

1 tablespoon plain gelatin
1 cup milk
1 egg
¼ cup sugar
1 teaspoon vanilla extract or brandy
  flavoring
1 bar (4 oz.) GHIRARDELLI SWEET
  CHOCOLATE
1 cup heavy whipping cream
5 ice cubes

In blender container, stir gelatin into ⅓ cup cold milk; let stand 5 minutes to soften. Heat remaining ⅔ cup milk until very hot; pour into blender container. Blending on low, add egg, sugar and vanilla. Chop chocolate into very small pieces; gradually add it to blended mixture. When chocolate has melted, add ice cubes, one at a time, blending until smooth. Pour in cream; blend on high. Let stand 10 minutes or until slightly thickened. Stir and pour into glass dessert dishes. Chill until firm. Garnish with additional whipped cream, if desired. Makes 6 (⅔ cup) servings.

Chilled or frozen . . . this perfect soufflé will never fall flat!

SEVEN HILLS FROSTY CHOCOLATE SOUFFLÉ

1 tablespoon plain gelatin
⅓ cup milk
1 package (6 oz.) GHIRARDELLI
  SEMI-SWEET CHOCOLATE CHIPS
2 tablespoons coffee liqueur
4 eggs, separated
⅔ cup sugar
Pinch salt
1 cup whipping cream

In double boiler, soak gelatin in milk until thickened. Place over pan with 1-inch simmering water to melt gelatin. Add Chocolate Chips and coffee liqueur. Heat mixture, stirring frequently until smooth.

Beat egg yolks, gradually adding ⅓ cup of the sugar. Beat until very thick and lemon colored. With wire whip, stir chocolate mixture quickly while adding egg yolks slowly. Cool 2–3 minutes until slightly thickened, stirring gently. (Mixture must be quite hot.)

Beat egg whites with salt until foamy. Gradually add remaining ⅓ cup sugar, beating until stiff peaks form. Blend ¼ of egg whites into chocolate. Pour chocolate mixture into large bowl. Place remaining egg whites on top and gently fold together. Fold in whipped cream.

Pour into 1½-quart soufflé dish, fancy bowl or 8 stemmed glasses. Chill until firm or cover and freeze. Decorate with Spirited Whipped Cream and shaved chocolate, if desired. Makes 8 servings.

SPIRITED WHIPPED CREAM

Whip 1 cup whipping cream with 2 tablespoon powdered sugar and 3 tablespoons crème de cacao. Use to decorate top of Seven Hills Frosty Chocolate Soufflé or other Chocolate dessert.

CHOCOLATE CHIFFON PIE

Follow recipe for Seven Hills Frosty Chocolate Soufflé. Let chill 5–10 minutes to thicken slightly. Fill prepared 8-inch chocolate or graham cracker crumb crust. Chill until firm.

Have fun with chocolate recipes . . .

FLOATING ANGEL ISLAND DESSERT

Meringue
8 (1 cup) egg whites (room
    temperature)
Pinch salt
¾ teaspoon cream of tartar
½ teaspoon vanilla
1¼ cups sugar
¼ cup chopped pecans

Meringue
With wire whip or electric mixer, beat egg whites with salt, cream of tartar and vanilla until foamy. Gradually add sugar, beating until stiff peaks form. Spread into buttered 9-inch square baking pan. Sprinkle with nuts. Set pan into larger pan with 1-inch hot water. Bake at 300°F for 1 hour or until lightly browned. Cool on wire rack ar room temperature. Cut into triangles; cross cut corner to corner into 4 large triangles; cut down centers to form 8 wedges.

Custard Sauce
1½ cups milk
½ cup half and half
1 cup sugar
Pinch salt
1 package (6 oz.) GHIRARDELLI
    SEMI-SWEET CHOCOLATE CHIPS
8 egg yolks, beaten

Custard Sauce
In heavy saucepan, heat milk, half and half, sugar and salt. Add Chocolate Chips, stirring frequently, until mixture is quite hot and slightly thickened. With wire whip, stir chocolate mixture quickly while adding egg yolks slowly. Cook until pudding thickens, stirring gently. Sprinkle lightly with sugar to prevent film. Cover and chill. Spoon chocolate sauce into glass dishes. Top with wedge of meringue. Makes 8 servings.

Traditional French pudding . . .

LAFAYETTE CHOCOLATE POTS DE CRÈME

½ cup milk
½ cup half and half
1 tablespoon sugar
½ bar (4 sections) GHIRARDELLI SEMI-SWEET CHOCOLATE
3 egg yolks
Dash salt
1 tablespoon crème de cacao

In heavy saucepan, scald milk and half and half with sugar. Add broken chocolate; stir frequently until chocolate completely melts and thickens slightly. (Mixture must be quite hot.) Beat egg yolks with salt until very thick. With wire whip, stir chocolate mixture quickly while adding yolks slowly. Add liqueur; stirring gently, cook 2–3 minutes until pudding thickens. Pour into small pots de crème cups or glass dishes. Cover and chill. Makes 4 (⅓ cup) servings.

149

Something really different . . .

BUFFET CHOCOLATE CREAM CHEESE

1 package (8 oz.) cream cheese (room temperature)
⅓ cup GHIRARDELLI GROUND CHOCOLATE
½ teaspoon vanilla

Using a spoon, blend cream cheese with Ground Chocolate and vanilla. Spread into small serving dish. Chill until firm. Serve with crackers or spread on nut bread. Delicious with fresh fruit.

The most popular recipe from Ghirardelli Square . . .

ROCKY ROAD CANDY

1 package (10 oz.) GHIRARDELLI
   MILK CHOCOLATE BLOCKS
1½ cups miniature marshmallows
½ cup chopped walnuts

In double boiler, melt broken chocolate squares over 1-inch simmering water, stirring constantly. In microwave, melt chocolate on MEDIUM 1½–2½ minutes, testing frequently for softness; stir to melt lumps. Remove from heat. Chocolate should not be too hot (100°–120° F). Stir in marshmallows and walnuts. Pour into buttered 9 by 5-inch metal loaf pan. Chill until firm. Let stand at room temperature for 5 minutes for easy removal. Turn over to loosen whole slab of candy. Cut into squares. Makes 18 pieces.

Have a ball with chocolate popcorn. Yummy good!

CHOCOLATE POPCORN BALLS

½ cup popcorn
1 package (6 oz.) GHIRARDELLI
  SEMI-SWEET CHOCOLATE CHIPS
½ cup light corn syrup
½ cup water
1 cup sugar
Pinch salt
2 tablespoons butter or margarine
¾ cup chopped walnuts

Pop popcorn according to package directions (approximately 3 quarts popped). In heavy saucepan, melt Chocolate Chips with corn syrup. Stir in water, sugar and salt; heat to boiling, without stirring. Cook until hard ball stage (245° F) or about 40 minutes. Remove from heat; blend in butter. Toss popcorn with nuts and syrup; cool slightly. Press into balls. Makes 16 (½ cup) balls.

153

Students enjoy this special treat after a hard day at school . . .

ALCATRAZ ROCKS

1 package (12 oz.) GHIRARDELLI
  SEMI-SWEET CHOCOLATE CHIPS
1 cup crunchy peanut butter
2 cups raisins

In double boiler, melt Chocolate Chips with peanut butter over 1-inch simmering water. Stir in raisins. Drop by heaping tablespoon onto waxed paper or paper baking cups. Chill until firm. Makes 22 rocks.

Perfect fudge with this easy method . . .

QUICK CHOCOLATE FUDGE

¾ cup canned evaporated milk
½ cup butter, cut into pieces
2 cups sugar
¼ teaspoon salt
1 package (12 oz.) GHIRARDELLI
   SEMI-SWEET CHOCOLATE CHIPS
2 cups miniature marshmallows
1 teaspoon vanilla
1 cup chopped walnuts

In saucepan, heat milk with butter until melted. Add sugar and salt, constantly until liquid starts to boil. Cook on low heat, stirring, for 2 minutes. Remove from heat. Mix in Chocolate Chips and marshmallows, beating until smooth and thick. Stir in vanilla and nuts. Spread into buttered 9-inch square pan. Chill 2 hours or until firm. Cut into squares. Makes 1½ pounds fudge.

154

The richest chocolate you have ever tasted . . .

REGAL CHOCOLATE CANDY TRUFFLES

1 bar (4 oz.) GHIRARDELLI
   SEMI-SWEET CHOCOLATE
3 tablespoons butter
1½ tablespoons Amaretto or Grand
   Marnier liqueur
2 tablespoons GHIRARDELLI
   GROUND CHOCOLATE

In double boiler, melt chocolate over 1-inch simmering water, stirring constantly. Remove from heat. Add butter, stirring until melted. Mix in liqueur. Chill until firm enough to shape into small oval pieces. Roll in Ground Chocolate. Age overnight in refrigerator. Serve as dessert with coffee or use as garnish for frosted cake. Makes 18 pieces.

Gather the family together for a fudge party in the kitchen . . .

OPERA HOUSE CHOCOLATE FUDGE

⅔ cup half and half
1 package (4 oz.) GHIRARDELLI
   UNSWEETENED BAKING
   CHOCOLATE
1 tablespoon light corn syrup
2 cups sugar
¼ teaspoon salt
1 tablespoon butter
1 teaspoon vanilla
¾ cup chopped walnuts

In heavy saucepan, heat half and half with broken chocolate, corn syrup, sugar and salt. Stir until smooth. Heat to boiling; lower heat. Cook on low heat, uncovered, without stirring, to soft ball stage (235° F) or about 35 minutes. Cool to lukewarm. Stir in butter and vanilla. Beat by hand until fudge thickens. Stir in nuts. Spread into buttered 8-inch square pan. Chill until set. Cut into 25 squares.

The candy nightcap . . .

BROADWAY BOURBON BALLS

1 package (6 oz.) GHIRARDELLI
    SEMI-SWEET CHOCOLATE CHIPS
2 tablespoons light corn syrup
⅓ cup Bourbon
2½ cups finely crushed vanilla
    wafers
1 cup finely chopped walnuts
½ tablespoons sugar
1 tablespoon GHIRARDELLI
    GROUND CHOCOLATE

In double boiler, melt chocolate with corn syrup and Bourbon over 1-inch simmering water. Stir in wafers, nuts and powdered sugar. Shape into balls, using one tablespoon each. Roll balls in mixture of sugar and Ground Chocolate. Age overnight. Store in tightly covered can. Keeps several weeks. Makes 40 balls.

MAIL ORDER FORM

GHIRARDELLI CHOCOLATE CO.
1111 139th Avenue
San Leandro, California 94578

Telephone orders may be placed by calling the following toll free numbers M–F 8 a.m.–9 p.m. Sat. 8 a.m.–5 p.m.:
1-800-972-5288 (California residents only) / 1-800-942-1885 (Illinois residents only) / 1-800-323-9429 (All other areas)

We will quote you the current assortment prices and expedite your order.
Please have the following information ready when you call:

Name _____

Address _____

City _____ State _____ Zip Code _____

Please check the type of card you are using, enter your card number and expiration date, and sign your name.
☐ MASTERCARD   ☐ AMERICAN EXPRESS   ☐ VISA

ACCOUNT NO.   MO.   YR.

SIGNED _____   CARD EXPIRES

		QUANTITY	PRICE
☐ Assortment 1	Fourteen bars of premium Ghirardelli Chocolate...........................		
☐ Assortment 2	The World's Largest Chocolate Bar (5 pounds)		
☐ Assortment 3	Three pounds of Ghirardelli's All Purpose Ground Chocolate and Cocoa....		
☐ Assortment 4	The revised Ghirardelli Chocolate Cookbook		
	TOTAL		

Make check or money order payable to GHIRARDELLI CHOCOLATE CO.
GUARANTEE: We guarantee your satisfaction, or we will gladly refund your money.
CUSTOMER SERVICE: Use our special customer service number, 415-483-6970, Monday through Friday between 8:30 A.M. and 4:30 P.M. Pacific Standard Time. Sorry, this is not a toll free number and we cannot accept collect calls.
SHIPPING TIME: Allow 4 to 6 weeks for delivery. We deliver via UPS wherever possible.

✳✳Chocolate cannot be shipped during hot weather months.✳✳

I f you wish to order by mail, please call our toll free number for current prices, then mail this form to Ghirardelli Chocolate Co., 1111 139th Avenue, San Leandro, California, 94578. Enclose a check or money order payable to Ghirardelli Chocolate Co., or charge your order to your credit card (fill out credit card information on the form included with instructions for telephone orders).

Friend's
Name _____

Address _____

City _____

State _____ Zip _____

Gift No.	Qty	Price Each	Hand. & Ship.	Total Amount
1				
2				
3				
4				
			SUBTOTAL	

Friend's
Name _____

Address _____

City _____

State _____ Zip _____

Gift No.	Qty	Price Each	Hand. & Ship.	Total Amount
1				
2				
3				
4				
			SUBTOTAL	

Friend's
Name _____

Address _____

City _____

State _____ Zip _____

Gift No.	Qty	Price Each	Hand. & Ship.	Total Amount
1				
2				
3				
4				
			SUBTOTAL	

Friend's
Name _____

Address _____

City _____

State _____ Zip _____

Gift No.	Qty	Price Each	Hand. & Ship.	Total Amount
1				
2				
3				
4				
			SUBTOTAL	

MAIL ORDER FORM

GHIRARDELLI CHOCOLATE CO.
1111 139th Avenue
San Leandro, California 94578

OFFICE INFORMATION AND
CODE AREA   CB

Telephone orders may be placed by calling the following toll free numbers M–F 8 a.m.–9 p.m. Sat. 8 a.m.–5 p.m.:
1-800-972-5288 (California residents only) / 1-800-942-1885 (Illinois residents only) / 1-800-323-9429 (All other areas)

We will quote you the current assortment prices and expedite your order.
Please have the following information ready when you call:

Name _____

Address _____

City _____ State _____ Zip Code _____

Please check the type of card you are using, enter your card number and expiration date, and sign your name.

☐ MASTERCARD ☐ AMERICAN EXPRESS ☐ VISA

ACCOUNT NO.

⬜⬜⬜⬜⬜⬜⬜⬜⬜⬜⬜⬜⬜⬜⬜⬜⬜⬜⬜⬜

MO.   YR.
⬜⬜
CARD EXPIRES

SIGNED _____

	Assortment	Description	QUANTITY	PRICE
☐	Assortment 1	Fourteen bars of premium Ghirardelli Chocolate...........................		
☐	Assortment 2	The World's Largest Chocolate Bar (5 pounds)		
☐	Assortment 3	Three pounds of Ghirardelli's All Purpose Ground Chocolate and Cocoa		
☐	Assortment 4	The revised Ghirardelli Chocolate Cookbook		
		TOTAL		

Make check or money order payable to GHIRARDELLI CHOCOLATE CO.
GUARANTEE: We guarantee your satisfaction, or we will gladly refund your money.
CUSTOMER SERVICE: Use our special customer service number, 415-483-6970, Monday through Friday between 8:30 A.M. and 4:30 P.M. Pacific Standard Time. Sorry, this is not a toll free number and we cannot accept collect calls.
SHIPPING TIME: Allow 4 to 6 weeks for delivery. We deliver via UPS wherever possible.
✱✱Chocolate cannot be shipped during hot weather months.✱✱

...u wish to order by mail, please call our toll free number for current prices, then mail this form to Ghirardelli ...olate Co., 1111 139th Avenue, San Leandro, California, 94578. Enclose a check or money order payable to ...rdelli Chocolate Co., or charge your order to your credit card (fill out credit card information on the form ...cluded with instructions for telephone orders).

Friend's
Name _____

Address _____

City _____

State _____ Zip _____

Gift No.	Qty	Price Each	Hand. & Ship.	Total Amount
1				
2				
3				
4				
			SUBTOTAL	

Friend's
Name _____

Address _____

City _____

State _____ Zip _____

Gift No.	Qty	Price Each	Hand. & Ship.	Total Amount
1				
2				
3				
4				
			SUBTOTAL	

Friend's
Name _____

Address _____

City _____

State _____ Zip _____

Gift No.	Qty	Price Each	Hand. & Ship.	Total Amount
1				
2				
3				
4				
			SUBTOTAL	

Friend's
Name _____

Address _____

City _____

State _____ Zip _____

Gift No.	Qty	Price Each	Hand. & Ship.	Total Amount
1				
2				
3				
4				
			SUBTOTAL	